THE CARNAGE MIRANDA LEAVES

*A High Schooler's Unmasked Struggle
with Trust, Lies, and Manipulation*

A. N. JACKSON

authorHOUSE®

AuthorHouse™
1663 Liberty Drive
Bloomington, IN 47403
www.authorhouse.com
Phone: 833-262-8899

Published by AuthorHouse 03/16/2023

ISBN: 978-1-6655-6578-3 (sc)
ISBN: 978-1-6655-6577-6 (e)

Library of Congress Control Number: 2022913470

Print information available on the last page.

This book is printed on acid-free paper.

Contents

Acknowledgments

I'd first like to express my gratitude to Jason, an experienced eye, who diligently read, helped edit, and gave critique to the many re-writes of this story. I am deeply grateful and I owe much to my brother, sister, parents, my grandmother, and Aunt Cynthia. They have always been great advocates while being present with their love, support, and wisdom throughout these years of writing this book.

I offer my gratitude for the guidance, insight, efforts, support, and talents that helped make this book come to be. My thanks extends to many, including: Christopher, Keenan, Fr. D. Mastrangelo, Rev. C. Drew, Paul, Kodie, Gabriella, Darnell, Deborah, Mammie, Abdullah, and Camilla. I also need to say thank you to P. Collison, who contributed his artistic talents by putting to canvas the cover art for this book.

Lastly, I'd like to acknowledge and encourage all those who've been exonerated, to continue the fight for those who remain unjustly convicted.

Chapter Review

Prologue

A poignant downcast of tears blare out and evokes an aching vibration throughout Axel's family home. After the anxious attempt is made to ease his mother from the true image of twelve jurors saying guilty to his older brother Nathan, Axel pours his attention to the welfare of his father and older sister Isabella. Meanwhile, the well-worn years of litigation has Nathan's defense team mute about aiding scheduled appeals. Nevertheless, Nathan soon finds out that his education was going to be the nucleus for future arguments, since his parents were weary about wagering another large sum of money on additional attorneys.

(1)
Chartered Privileges:

Venturing back to the framework of Axel's mother's side of the family, the makeup of Nathan's jury draws deeply on an age old paralleling family civil suit. Later, South Carolina becomes home for Axel and Isabella. No faster than their school semester begins, an extra credit assignment on civil liberties and constitutional rights sends Axel to start studying the amendment affecting his brother. As the history of what he learns helps with the boost of a grade, his mother later breaks down in laymen terms, the legal aspects of what Nathan's attorneys spent so much time challenging.

(2)
Committing Time:

Resolved on getting Isabella to grow aware of America's safeguarding liberties, both siblings go for a walk on their property where they bask in their heart-tugging feelings about Nathan's mitigated whereabouts. To fuel the position of not waiting on a miracle to happen, Axel convinces his sister to help him find the truth amongst their family's disaster. Their mother sees the desired movement as a rhythm that will beat low majority of the time, but Axel is convinced that the woman who brought him into this world will turn out to be one of the most powerful weapons in his arsenal. During this interval of time of trying to figure out specific steps forward, Nathan receives a letter from his brother then gives a response that's meant to tear down Axel's embolden idea.

(3)
Future In Disguise:

Following a peek into two high profile cases that help Nathan's ordeal develop a selective deafness amongst the media, Axel weaves a tale about his brother's cultured life. As Nathan ascends his knowledge at one of Detroit's prominent Catholic High Schools, a growth of viable friendships grow while he engages in a long love connection with the daughter of a socialite judge. When conflict ensues about a problematic family quarrel, the birthplace of Jazz becomes Nathan's seasonable place to temporarily live. Then after graduation, a year of college, and a job at an automotive parts plant, Lake Buena Vista, Florida welcomes Nathan as a new employee at the whimsical Walt Disney World.

(4)
Demanding Voices:

The brick and mortar exterior of Jackson State Penitentiary drops out of sight when Axel and his mother stepped inside to visit Nathan. When the grandeur of their reunification draws down, Axel settles comfortably when the immediacy of his mother's voice demands Nathan to explain what she already knows.

(5)
Mayhem:

Nathan transforms his conversation with Axel and begins to shed light on the well supported details concerning his arrest. The story drives their mother to reveal chilling facts of Nathan's trial to Axel. As the chin dropping dialogue persists, the visit with Nathan is cut short. But before they leave, Axel wants answers about what contributed to the surprisingly victims' death.

(6)
Reflections:

Axel brings into question his family's disposition of care in a family matter.

(7)
Waiving Away Safeguards:

Axel and his brother have a chance to speak about the constitutional pitfalls Nathan is battling. Axel becomes confined with Nathan's discussion on the importance of Miranda Rights. After the main points of this history lesson, an account of Nathan's experience with police in an interrogation room is divulged. When the thought-provoking facts of his interrogation come out, Axel starts to analyze the overt measures surrounding the investigator's practices amongst his brother's interrogation.

(8)
Inspiration:

Before Switzerland is visited to see family, Axel's grandmother responds to the skepticism about what she witnessed at Nathan's trial. Later, a break for timeless memories become center stage before Axel jumps into a four month research regimen of his brother's court documents. Soon after he learns about the millions of dollars won in the victim's settlement, Axel is self-posed to the belief that there could be another motive on part of whoever was responsible. At a final peruse of reports and transcripts, crucial evidence is found to have not been tested for DNA.

(9)
Enlightening Arguments:

Foreshadowing the emphasis of the Michigan Court of Appeals ruling, Axel is enticed to begin a self-exploration, much the same as his brother tries to achieve. But when barriers get in the way of survival inside prison, sheer exhaustion motivates a call out for help. Quickly, Axel dives into Nathan's recent arguments to the court about his deprivation of State and Federal rights against self-incrimination and due process. In viewing the prosecutor's response, Axel discovers another Constitutional violation which is separate from the un-valid waiver of Nathan Miranda's rights.

(10)
Tactical Disadvantage:

The magic of Axel's headway produces a skillful test which demonstrates how the courts determine the presence of coercive law enforcement behavior amongst interrogative circumstances. As time passes, the anecdote that seems to be inscribed in the keeping with state laws, Axel exemplifies the impact with his brother's case. Suddenly, a mystery of mechanics help make an interconnection that taps into the aggressive research of how and why innocent people acknowledge guilt for crimes they have not committed. Coming after the productive interaction concerning therapeutic remedies for curing coercive police methods, Axel makes an aggressive response.

(11)
Transparency:

Axel sparks a narrative about the combined possibilities for change in police departments. His internal will wants to hire a linguistics' professional to assess Nathan's case. Axel realizes though, a recording of Nathan's interrogation would have went a long way in proving a constitutional claim.

(12)
A Brazen Commitment:

Axel waits to hear how the Michigan Supreme Court will rule on Nathan's issues. Undeterred by the possibilities of bad news, Axel knows a petition to the federal courts will be managed. If all fails, the Innocence Project could take over before Nathan makes a decision to motion his trial court once more. In the time between, Axel bends towards the conclusion with a symphonic message meant to bring about awareness throughout our nation.

To my parents, who have always been instrumental at helping transcend my ideas beyond routine.

Author's Note:

This book is based on a true story. The opinions written herein should not be a substitute for any kind of legal or psychological analysis given by licensed professionals. Every effort has been made to ensure that the presented law agencies are accurate. To protect their privacy, the names of family, friends, associates, and some law officials, have all been changed to pseudonyms.

Prologue

It was day two...December 22, 2004, to be exact. An unarmed conflict between two territorial divides had reached the point of finality the day before. There was nothing left to do but wait on Judge McDonald's courtroom to return back from adjournment. Anxiously, both sides found themselves waiting in the courtroom, hoping their clever showmanship paid off.

Given the enormous buildup of implicit biases that shapes America's justice system, Axel thought his family's jubilation was a bit premature. All sorts of emotions were to be had, but the fast paced thrumming of his heart-beat, while watching each juror take a turn towards their seats in the courtroom is what brought on a deep stillness that attached onto everyone inside.

Not remembering if he heard them, or just saw the emotions plastered on spectators' faces, but the reactions were quick when the news came in. The sequence of images unfolding had Axel becoming delusional, with endless suffering, or perhaps a slow death. What, if anything, was beyond the darkened space he found himself in. He had no clue. When the worst of those thoughts left Axel, he woke from the overwhelming forces, then realized what was being doled out was heartbreaking truths that encompassed details he wished would miraculously disappear.

For a few minutes there was a disconnect from the world. Axel was a young, slim, beardless middle-schooler, cave-dwelling in the refuge of a dimly lit bedroom closet. This was seriously a true and devastating reality no kid should have to accustom themselves to. Tears of pain which manifested into a secession of guttural cries, quickly became muffled when Axel slid an arm full of sports apparel toward both sides of his face. The forcefulness of his accelerated facial change, vividly expressed the non-celebratory mood he was in. Time alone for grieving is what was needed, it was especially what his family needed.

The less Axel understood, he believed, robbed him of what actually occurred with the young man who was a part of his life since birth. It was not the time to closely examine particulars, but the day for such revelation would soon come, he thought. First, a momentum had to be built in order to rise out beyond the opaque space he put himself in. When an ushering of encouragement lifted Axel's body from the dismal stance, his flushed lenses acted like a telescope while zeroing in on what was happening outside. From his bedroom window he noticed how the sky was just about done dusting the tree lined street with the fine powdery snow that came to his Northwest Detroit neighborhood every winter.

All three fireplaces in his home created a relaxing ambiance throughout the spacious brick colonial, and the heat flowing from each one of them helped peek his core many degrees past normal. The first inclination, he thought, was to wind the window open and allow the crisp air to cool himself down. Then, a change in mind came and he opted not to do so. Instead, he began a slow stride and ended up putting his thin arms into a knitted sweater. This provided a level of warmth for taking a leisurely stroll around his peaceful neighborhood.

The brief period of time it took Axel to touch base with the patio door, his forward progress was forced to a dead stop. He turned his head towards the noise and kept a wondering glance while his eyes widened as if to say, "What is that?" Something unpleasant kept vibrating the walls, and there was no way he was leaving without making sure everything was fine. Ultimately, Axel's radar went off in front of his parents' bedroom door.

Inching his ear onto the surface of the sunken square panel door, his attention peaked even more when he heard his mother let out another steel rubbing moan. Desperately, Axel rushed through the molded doorframe, where he noticed the beautiful woman who brought him into this world. She was succumbing to a mental pang, while curled up like a fetus underneath her comforter. All he could do was climb into her bed and stroke the side of her body that was raised with the covers.

"It's going to be okay," Axel voiced, not knowing exactly how his elicitation would even convince her to stop the taxing out pour of emotions.

Telling by his mother's tempo, she had more to expel. Across the hall, he went to check on his older sister Isabella. She was flattened out like she'd fell from a cliff. Her straight hair was ruffled, but it cascaded off the side of her bed like the ends of a frayed blanket. She was drained for the same reasons as everyone else, but Axel was glad to see she was out like a prize fighter because Isabella and her mother crying at the same time would have been too much for his ears. The only soul who hadn't expressed their sentiment was Axel's strong willed father. On this saddened day his father seemed to hold onto his pride and put on a face to disguise the raw pain inside. His bulgy, dark brown eyes, had become dispirited.

Once hearing the eldest son's circumstances was the cause of everyone's weeping session, Axel's father's body language exuded somewhat of a nothingness.

"What say the jury?" the judge asked.

"In the case of the *People v Nathan Henson,* we the jury find the defendant, Guilty."

Barbed wire; handcuffs; body searches; police harassment; gangs; peer pressures; ill-equipped law libraries; and poor medical care was now Axel's nineteen-year-old brother's reality. Did Nathan's dream team of attorneys pledge a sense of loyalty to him? Did Nathan's representatives honestly believe in saving him? Or was it about acquiring billable hours? To impress a belief upon a client is one thing, but to actually make good on a strategy is multi-dimensional in itself, and that takes dedication and grit.

While Axel had witnessed firsthand how Nathan had a depth of knowledge beyond his years, he also knew other than a participation in an Explorers class at the corporate law firm their mother worked at, in his opinion, Nathan had no skill to take on his liberty interest all by himself. Especially when the average law student takes a total of eight plus years to understand rules, procedures, constitutional law, and argument strategies. It would be incongruous however, to conclude that anyone who doesn't attend law school, would be able to learn such a complex subject, Axel thought.

The ability to go outside ones comfort zone in order to pursue education for reasons of understanding and applicability, brought thoughts of individuals like Lebron James, Oprah, and Richard Branson, who were all ambitiously driven to success without much of a formal education. Many pioneers have paved a legitimate passage way for millions, and their pledge is what Axel hoped Nathan would inject into his life for the sake of what devotion could bring him.

Besides, Nathan had to figure out something suitable to tackle the maze-like intricacies he would be faced with. Because the days of him getting extra funds for another set of attorneys seemed to be over after his parents wasted tens of thousands of dollars for a verdict that belongs to corrupt officials who never get charged.

Axel was young, uncertain, and uneducated about whether or not Nathan's case was full of constitutional violations in favor of trapping and putting away an array of people, including the rich. What was of no confusion is the pursuit Axel aims for. It was an internal will. A determined attempt at helping reverse Nathan's conviction is what was going to fulfill Axel moving forward. He desires to be the hero who saves the innocent. He wants to be the greatest son, a reliable brother, and a fun friend. Often Axel departs from the routine, primarily because Nathan's story would not go anywhere without telling the narrative himself.

1

Chartered Privileges

Was it fear of the local law officials in the suburbs of Detroit that made me view the future with alarm? Or, were they the ones who helped strengthen my will? Oakland County has a historic reputation as being one of America's richest counties with an eerie past. Before the time of wreckage and removal of culturally sensitive statutes, suburban development for the purpose of hyper-local governance became popular. The separation among communities that are merely a stone's throw away from each other seemed to rise fast after citizens became the surplus of commodities for state prisons. Now, my brother Nathan was a statistic of both.

The relative wealth of Michigan's prominent county is sourced by gated enclaves of professionals who juggle two or more flashy homes just to represent how much power they have. And just like those who look to live in exceptional locations, my grandparents, bought homes that sat amid the most desirable addresses of their city.

Family gatherings were enjoyed behind long private wrap-around driveways at stunning home-sites, where the serene landscapes served as a polaroid shot to the memories I have.

Specifically, my grandparents' estate was a spacious place with tons of comfort, but the décor screamed opulence. The taste was solely my grandmother's, and it always seemed like my grandfather had no say in the choices made inside the home. None of that mattered to him I take it. I say that for a number of reasons, primarily because my grandfather was the one who ultimately sacrificed himself for some of his family's prestige.

As my mother and her siblings, two sisters and one brother, went off to college to obtain prestigious careers, justice for an accident that claimed one of my grandfather's appendages ended after a long litigation battle. July 1974, was when my grandfather's glove was caught on a conveyor belt at a Chrysler Plant he worked at. His right arm and shoulder were pinched between a belt and turning drum. There was no undoing the damage done. But he countered it and his attorney hailed the verdict against a Fabricating company. It was a step in establishing manufacturers' responsibility nationwide. The jury consisting of eleven women and one man awarded my grandparents tax free money that turned a liability into assets, and would last for generations.

With my mother starting her long career at a corporate law firm in downtown Detroit, her wedding to my father was one of those things my grandparents invested well in. Although I personally don't have memories of the huge ceremony, because I was not born yet, I look back at old snapshots and see how exciting of a time everyone was having. When I look into the eyes of Nathan, who was all of five years old in those pictures then, I see the necessity of his being.

As highly publicized as my grandfather's accident was, my brother's criminal case attracted many spectators as well. Unlike the engineering company that had the obligation of paying my mother's parents, Nathan received a decision of life imprisonment without the possibility of parole, from the same jury make-up as my grandfather had in his civil trial.

It was weeks after a permanent wall was erected between my brother and his freedom, when I absorbed a phone conversation between Nathan and our father. Some of those words continue to be embedded in my mind, even though I didn't know what the context really meant at the time. Making sense out of chaos was not my dad's expertise, but he was confused about the maddening complicated issues dealing with one of the Amendments and how a law attached with those protections allowed for such treatment. Nathan, with his new found love of the law, emphasized to us how the courts' erroneous ruling was going to be difficult to overcome, but our dad didn't think it would be too difficult. Positive action had to start with my brother stopping his pervasive and abiding distrust for the justice system as a whole, my dad explained to Nathan.

When the fifty-foot concrete walls engulfed my brother's physical self, Isabella and I were relocated to South Carolina where we moved into a house our parents had built when Nathan was going through his legal battles. The plan was for us all to move into our brand new home, but no sooner before we could settle in comfortably, our father was called to Minnesota for a contract job where he worked as a systems engineer.

It seemed like the ghost of ill-fortune continued to plague Isabella and I. When my father's mother changed her residence to live with us, our mother revealed she was filing for divorce and wasn't planning on joining us permanently.

While the thought of my parents being separated did bring teary-eyes on days, my first year of high school approached and just maybe, I hoped, the negative emotions I was experiencing could be converted into my love for sports. My baseball and football coaches at St. John's High were instrumental in helping me settle the battle of my emotional upheaval which came from the slow deterioration of my family. Their presence with helping me through my pain paid off. Ultimately, my performance on both fields reached an all-time high. So much so that before I knew it journalists were writing articles about me while I kept being introduced to college scouts.

"If there's any clear way to wake a person up about an issue at hand," said my coach. "There's no need to yell at them. Why not just splash cold water on their faces to wake them up to the situation. Not literally though." That's exactly what happened when I tried dozing off during history class one afternoon.

The day I speak of, my teacher was remarking that "Society's concept of 'we the people,' has changed." During his lecture I learned that the yellowed Constitution of America, which the Bill of Rights came from, was about to turn two hundred and eighteen years old. My teacher urged us to study anything we wanted on civil liberties and constitutional rights. Afterwards, he wanted those interested in participating, to draft a report about whether we believe the language in the living documents he referred to were in line with today's evolution.

Perhaps I thought along the lines of abandoning the extra credit, but the heartfelt talk my dad and Nathan had would haunt my thoughts if I did. Even though this report would not repair the damage of injustices so many had shouted about, I recognized the courage not to give up on the difficult questions law makers today continue to propagate their opinions about. Besides, it was another moment for me to showcase why Detroit's ex-mayor, who himself was bequeathed a long prison sentence, chose me as the winner of a city wide writing contest two years before.

In the late night hours that warm weekend, I sat at my computer and printed out both charters of liberties. With the exception of the intricate words I needed to look up in a dictionary in order to tackle my literary composition, I called my dad and had him remind me which Amendment Nathan had a vested interest in challenging.

"The Fifth Amendment," he said.

My mood had adjusted to a more devoted interest by then, and when I found myself leaning into the living structure that for hundreds of years has resonated through America's history, I honored the take command attitudes of our founding fathers considering the odds they were against. Chunks of our chronicled narratives create images of Benjamin Franklin and the remaining framers of the United States Constitution, as grey haired men. The truth is, many of these creators were predominantly young, educated, former soldiers, politicians, some were considerably wealthy, and many were slave owners.

These men also looked to create a national supremacy where the preclusion of citizens inalienable rights were delegated by individualized state constitutions. To put it plainly, the United States Constitution was authority, but sovereign states who opposed such federalized guarantees could ignore those protections and embrace their own interest.

It wasn't until three years after President Lincoln's assassination, and three years after the abolishment of slavery, when the viability of states sovereignty flat-lined. In accordance with the ratification of the U.S. Constitution that year, all states were forced to adhere to the emergence of our Fourteenth Amendment. There was an all across the board ban on abridging privileges of citizens in the United States. Nor could a state forbid any person of life, liberty or property, without due process of law or equal protection of those laws.

To write decently on my assignment surrounding the Fifth Amendment and how it applied in real life circumstances, I had to clear my mind of all the distractions, then get back to focusing on the boldface text lingering in my hand. My eyes read the First Amendment, while my index finger found the Fifth Amendment.

I couldn't help but think about how my writing would measure up to my classmates. Still, I seized the moment and worked like an author while detailing the miscarriage of justice connected with a few illegal ways authorities go about violating citizens due process rights.

One by one the following Monday afternoon, each student who elected to participate in the assignment went before the class and read their reports. Instead of writing about either original document, one of my classmates wrote about the process of how Amendments from the Constitution get drafted and put into State Constitutions. He went further to explain that after representatives of the legislature approves a bill, his parents told him most times citizens were being persecuted with loopholes that committees refuse to patch up. Another classmate spoke about everyone's right to privacy and how those essential rights are constantly being challenged every possible way.

Then there was Jennifer. She was tall, approachable, out spoken, and pretty. She stood in view of all the students and spoke about her aunt's fight for same sex marriage. While many argued marrying the same sex is against the very fabric of America, Jennifer's aunt argued that the Constitution forbids all discrimination.

After everyone read what they compiled, I wondered if other schools across our country had ever taught students about their rights and the importance of them in relation to the consistency of life today. As I'd realized, if it weren't for the extra credit I did, my understanding of the Constitution's applicability would be poor. And even after I grasped somewhat of an understanding, I still didn't know ten percent of its worth.

Later that evening, I spoke with my mother concerning the presentation I felt I was being viewed suspicious about. Her consensus of the information in my speech served my need for a pat on the back, but her beacon of light shortly after astonished me. In that moment, I regretted not consulting her days prior. What I put down in writing had not even touched the surface of the grand issues connected to a state authority my brother needed to press the gas pedal down on and contest.

Regardless to the fact that I was a teen who wanted to romanticize with the idea of endless fun, I also knew that history judges us by our actions. I knew all too well that my brother's fate had been determined, and despite impressions from people who weren't in his shoes, nor in my shoes, or anyone in our family's shoes, I wanted to go the distance and search for the vaccine which would eradicate the accelerated rate of behavior that threatened citizens' will and freedoms. So I envisioned a strategy where I would dip my feet in the water and travel aside those well-known organizations that had integrated this moral authority to overhaul nontransparent laws and procedures which the courts turn a blind eye to. First though, I needed to muster the courage and talk with Nathan about the day he found himself in a world of trouble.

2

Committing Time

Back in the familiar surroundings of my comfortable bedroom in Charleston, South Carolina, I began realizing how no one expected me to recognize the changes that were occurring. I figured an unavoidable consequence would soon follow if the wind of despair did not shift. Stress, addiction, family division, lack of faith, and possibly even physical deterioration were all super-storm ailments strong enough to shatter the shield my family hid behind. How could I ever allow for a court system to rule the emotions of me and my family even though Nathan was under their jurisdiction.

An oil painting came to mind and gave me encouragement when I would catch myself surrendering to the waves of sentimental impressions that reminded me of my family's emotional wounds. These reflections take me back to summers in Durant, Oklahoma. There were no crowds, no strangers, and no disturbances. The only issue that stood out was the lack of diversity in terms of racial population.

Later in life, I'd learned how my parents and grandparents had not given me an education on Oklahoma's significant events. Particularly, in a neighborhood called Greenwood, blacks in Tulsa created a rich, viable business and residential district that had a fashionable name. Black Wall Street was what the African American developers called the region. In 1921, a Black man was wrongly accused of assaulting a Caucasian woman in an elevator. As he stepped onto the elevator, the man tripped, and in the process of falling he grabbed ahold of the woman to gain balance. Her clothes were ripped and the elevator operator saw it as an assault. Later that day, a mob of white natives looted and destroyed most of the black owned businesses. This is why, I assumed, there was such a gap in diversity throughout the state.

The trips to Durant and neighboring cities were long and boring if we weren't at our grandparents, or at the Frontier Amusement Park. Each year I looked forward to taking pictures in front of the cathedral size columns on the porch of my grandparents' replica plantation style vacation home. After I would be done snapping my disposable cameras, I would walk through the eight foot doors and instantly catch sight of an art piece. It rested in silence off to the side of the foyer. I've not always paid close attention to it though. Most times I'd walk pass the easel to go look at the panoramic views of the country land from the back porch. It wasn't until a certain day when the framed piece began to be regarded as a profound example of what my mother's parents conquered in order to give us the life we were living.

"I need ya'll in here," my mom voiced.

She sounded like a journalist reading off a sensational headline to the world. Nathan, Isabella, and I, lost no time in seeing what she wanted. We met at the front of the curved staircase where she stood. Her eyes were scurrying the array of earth tones that made up the rustic shack painted on the square canvas.

"Any of you know what this is?" she asked, looking straight at us with her hand modeling atop of the trimmed painting.

I thought I knew the answer but I never responded. The textured illustration awakened me to the thought of it being our paternal great-grandmother's home who was brought up in a similar place in Monroeville, Alabama.

"Your grandparents raised us in that house," she told us emphatically.

My mother went on explaining that her parents and siblings lived there before moving to Michigan. The crudely built house was surprisingly still standing.

"Can we go see it?" I remember asking, as if wanting to take a trip to the arcade.

"If we find time," my mom said, "we will."

Authenticity; adversity; love; memories; sacrifice; and victory, are all deep seeded expressions that embodied what that painting began symbolizing from that day forward.

Arranging each of those qualities in my mind, body, and spirit, would be fundamental to the movement I was planning to put in place for Nathan. Regardless of the fact that my brother's equanimity about his situation was not consistent with what so many thought was proper, I could not allow anything or anyone to strike down my efforts before I could even get started. Now, all I needed to know was if Isabella could find time in her busy schedule to help me take the stance against officers from having had disenfranchised our brother and so many other vulnerable individuals.

It was mid May of 2006 at this juncture and all my sister's attention floated throughout the room, only to then return to the excitement surrounding prom, high school graduation, and traveling abroad before college. Isabella never ceased to amaze me with her taste for worldly possessions, which we all as kids sought after. But subsequent to me hearing her conversation over the phone about the scale of her dress and what her date would be driving for the special occasion, I summoned Isabella to come walk outside with me so we could spend some time together.

We stretched our feet to the last step of our deck and started to walk side by side towards the yard space where we had acres of wooded area to roam before we ran into a waterway. All of four foot ten at seventeen, my sister was, I wrapped my arm around her small shoulders and we started to toddle along the pathway of our property at a leisurely pace.

I was cognizant of the fact that she might say school was occupying the bulk of her time. Even though the same was true for me too, I was sure to somehow make an effort at helping free Nathan no matter what it took. If Isabella did use such a weak defense, well, I assumed I would come up with something creative to get her on board with my idea.

Before I could really think about all of what I needed to say, my tongue got ahead of me. I looked down at the side of her face and asked, "You think you have the courage to go to war for Nathan?" I have to admit, my statement sounded more like I was trying to have her join some type of militia so that she could physically break him out of prison. My sister tilted her head at me, while squeezing the skin in between her eyes tightly together. Her posture spoke a million words. Her eyes as I had always known them to be, quickly started showing signs of a sympathetic response. The infinite mercy she believed in, was going to lay his protective hands on Nathan and save him from the tough trials in life, she explained.

"But we all know it takes more than just believing in the workings of God. We have to put forth some type of effort as well," I said in a slight tone of authority.

At that point, I recognized she needed to be given a more astute observation of some of the things I inherited while doing research for my history paper. With a catalogue of inquisitions I wanted my sister to filter through, I began to test her knowledge as we made our way towards the sound of the river a couple acres ahead of us.

"Ask yourself," I began while separating my arm from her shoulder so I could push aside a large tree branch that was in our way. "Why did slavery take so long to be abolished?"

Isabella shrugged her shoulders as if to say she didn't care for the subject. I knew she at least had an opinion.

"Look at me for a second will you."

I think she was stunned by my inflection, but her head quickly turned in my direction.

"Do you believe we can break the rules of pursuing what we want to be, and instead get involved with areas that will shape the way our kids will live?"

Isabella was speechless. I could tell the traffic in her head was heavy, but I continued throwing questions at her.

"And how long did it take poor people, minorities, and immigrants to fight and receive equality in this country?"

Her response was to the point. "People are still struggling for fair treatment on a lot of issues."

"Okay, like what?"

"Like abortion, voting rights, and the right to privacy."

"Now, do you believe change in laws and policies are solely in the hands of citizens or representatives of our state and federal governments?"

"There's committees who have to vote on bills representatives bring to the floor."

"Where do these ideas that representatives bring to the floor come from?" I asked.

"People of the community."

"That's right! But should our liberties be compromised by authorities who are sworn to uphold and protect the law?"

"Of course not, but what do we do?" Isabella asked with cluelessness in her voice.

"If we were to reverse roles with government officials and apply the old saying of, 'do unto others as we would have them do unto us,' would that be enough of a payment for their unequitable rules?"

I could not tell whether Isabella was open to answering the question truthfully. I believe she was thinking of a safe way to respond. So, I kept expounding on what I was convinced of while we continued walking.

"Taking a circular saw to the chains on Nathan's wrists is what we need to do." I said with my tone seeming overrated.

I wanted Isabella to be moved by my passion like she is when she hears a preacher deliver a sermon. What do you say in response to the facts about miscreant law personnel hired in the justice system today? That's exactly how my sister's face registered before her deep stillness made a break. She started expressing how in today's fast break society it's all too common for us to pass each other by without a second glance.

"Often times I know I get a little or no time at all to consider what's even going on with Nathan," Isabella paused for a few seconds then continued. "So for you to be interested in something so adult, I kind of feel like the roles here are reversed."

She went on remarking that she could not fathom the idea of our brother staying caged up forever. Although she believed justice would still come in the path of some type of spiritual happening, she did not want me to feel like I was all on my own. When I heard those expressions from her, we had already stopped at the waters' edge.

"Traveling and college won't get in the way. I promise!" she said seriously.

I couldn't hold it anymore. With desperation and urgency, I scooped Isabella from the ground and gave her a vice-like hug like she's never had before.

As the outside landscape started to recede into a blur, we backtracked pass all the mature mossy oak trees and went home. Before we entered, I gave Isabella a bit of my own spiritual knowledge just to keep in the back of her mind.

"Be mindful of the people that can be salvaged because you never know what waits for us when we take notice of others, before we care for ourselves."

Isabella turned to look at me to say, "You're right! That's a truth we all should pay attention to."

I must admit, my sister and I were on auto-pilot most of our time in South Carolina. At times I worried a lot if maybe Nathan began to resent us because we had not written or even so much as spoken to him over the phone for some time. I was sure there was no semblance of normalcy for him behind those barbed wires. However, when I wanted to know how he was holding up, I would call our mother to find out.

Maybe Nathan was a smidgen confused about why he hadn't heard from us. But I told our mother though, the next time she were to talk with Nathan, to let him know there were lessons to be drawn from his life, and that Isabella and I wanted to help be tyrant forces who dismantled the injustice done to him. With little apprehension, my mother pointed out some of the objections I would get while trying to prevail on the unfair treatment and procedures specific to my brother's situation. Her thoughts were, "you'd be in over your head."

Then, my mother burst off over the phone about how the youth of this country love basking in un-economic articles such as video games, social media, sports, and entertainment. She was proud of my direction. Our exchange turned into a discussion about how we needed a more informed democracy. In specific, separating ourselves from understanding policies of the law simply because we don't like the subject or because we don't understand it, makes us absolutely vulnerable to the people who create and enforce the laws.

Not all in my generation, my mother and I agreed, had a hard time accepting constructive criticism about themselves. Some were just too easily offended though. "If we do not transcend this attitude so that we can be a better class of people who defy explanation, then we will always be held in bondage," she said emphatically.

With me assuming leadership of the wagering fight ahead, I figured there were plenty sparing partners to keep me in shape. I suspected my mother would put her reputation on the line for me and call in a favor or two if or when the time came around. While I began my first stages in pursuit of information about my brother's case, my mother said she would buy me a plane ticket to Michigan after my sister's graduation, so I could go and speak with Nathan at the prison he was in. Before then, I was eager to send him a letter of encouragement. When I bordered the last paragraph, I concluded my final words:

> *"Anger is leveraged towards the three Pee's, (police, prosecutors, and politicians) because of un-confronted issues. While I don't know all the specifics, it's a must we speak on those facts when I come up in a couple of weeks. After listening to mom talk about those detectives in your case using illegitimate methods which Michigan*

> *State Laws supposedly upholds, I was mad, hell*
> *I was pissed. I just want you to know that if*
> *anyone is going to try and make a change for*
> *you, it's your family."*
>
> *With Love,*
> *Your Brother - - - - - -*

Eight days exactly, I walked to the end of my driveway to get the mail. My pledge to Nathan must've excited him because he responded back quicker than I anticipated. Anxious to know what all he said in reply, I broke open the gummed seal and unfolded the single sheet of paper. From start to finish Nathan's words hit me right in the gut. To sum his reply up, it was combustible. Nathan mentioned how court officials were a bunch of dangerous adversaries who would only listen to my arguments for the time during which it took to get from one floor on an elevator to the next.

More than anything, I felt Nathan did not believe he was ever going to make it out of his ordeal. It was important for me and my family to change this thinking. In the meantime, I only had another five days until I were to see my brother. In the time between, I gave thought to Nathan's life when he was free.

3

Future in Disguise

I magine the disappointment of finding out the person you were being raised with, isn't who you believed them to be. Instead of being disgruntled, I was shocked to learn, at the age of eight, what Nathan's lineage was. When I learned of this news, I felt like I was being stripped of the one possession I enjoyed so much. Come to think of it, I'd looked with contempt at the scathing revelations.

My mother's statement was crippling until my dad's voice said, "Axel...I might not have my blood running through your brother, but you do. No matter what, I will always be his father." This was no overstatement. Months following my parent's marriage, my dad and Nathan were returning home late one night when they became victims of a brazen attack at a busy intersection. As I grew up, I heard the heart plummeting story of how the men blocked my dad in, jumped out their car with bats, and emptied all their road rage aggression onto my dad's prized Volkswagen Jetta.

The assailants showed no sign of righteousness as they looked in Nathan's five-year-old eyes while ruining the side of the car with each whack. As the seconds kept ticking, things got worse. A rapid "THWACK! THWACK! THWACK!" sounded out as shards of glass poured over Nathan's crouched body. At the front of the car, one of the strangers stood on the hood and slammed the bat into the windshield as if he was trying to break up concrete with a sledge hammer.

Thankfully, neither Nathan or my dad were physically harmed. It's hard to imagine the personal devastation that came to them in my dad's car that night, but it fed into other areas that made them close. So much so that, when Nathan started high school, he and our mother legally changed his last name from Harrell to Henson. He was officially under my father's name.

At the age of twenty-six, my mother, Caraline Harrell and Franck Lyon, Nathan's biological father, met and attended Wayne State University in the city of Detroit. On November 16, 1983, my brother was born. Our mother and Franck weren't on good terms much of my brother's time in the womb, so she opted to give Nathan her name. As one can imagine, this caused a massive explosion. Franck did what he could to win our mother's heart again. He took the steps at beginning a career as an Automotive Engineer, but he struggled keeping his career because of alcoholism. Our mother on the other hand, began her long legal career, while in college as a legal secretary of a large corporate law firm in downtown Detroit.

While studying for his Automotive Excellence License, Franck labored his way as a welder at a Cadillac plant in order to have more time with Nathan. That didn't last long though. One of my mother's tipping points was when Catalina, Franck's newly-wed wife, mistakenly pushed Nathan into a table, causing a permanent mark to be embedded into the back of Nathan's head. Then, when Franck did pass the bar, two years later in the state of Louisiana, Nathan couldn't continue visiting his dad in New Orleans as he often had.

Eventually, Franck found himself involved in fraudulent schemes that land him in the hands of the government. Franck's unsavory actions landed him a first class flight to jail for a duration of almost two years. It didn't stop there though... officials at the detention center began disseminating Franck as being the ring leader of recruiting convicts to amass wealth, using methods the federal government frowned upon. As a consequence, Franck was shipped far from those who were able to visit him.

Throughout all the agitations, our mother never sought sole custody of Nathan, even when prison became Franck's reality. When the stress periods died down, Nathan was allowed back to visit his paternal grandmother and the rest of his family in Louisiana. But something was different in Nathan's attitude. The absence of his dad caused him to misbehave.

Jefferson Parish was the first place Nathan got into a physical altercation with someone of his own age. I have to make mention of how he was all of nine years old, at the time, when his pet turtle was stolen by twin brothers who lived in his uncle's neighborhood. Either Nathan would go get the turtle back, his uncle told him, or he would be punished for allowing the theft of something he played no part in paying for. The initial plea, with his so called friends, did not go over well. Nathan hurried back home with his head held down the entire way. Instead of going into the house to accept his judgment, my brother grabbed a broom on the covered back porch, then headed back down the street.

"I want my turtle back," Nathan yelled, at the same time he swung the broom at the two boys.

Although both brothers ran around taunting Nathan, eventually Nathan grabbed hold of the smallest brother and went upside his head with his fist like kids do. His actions warranted the results he'd been looking for all along. Nathan walked away proud with his turtle in hand.

By sixth grade, the world opened up to Nathan extremely fast. Credit is due to a neighborhood girl named Alicia, who introduced him to material inappropriate for a kid his age. She was a grade ahead of my brother, and before long the two of them were renewed to explore more as they watched pornographic movies together. I find it incredibly difficult to imagine the scenario because not only is it inappropriate for two kids to be interacting sexually, but during those times no one could fathom the thought of T-ball playing Nathan, committing such a sin so young. My brother's secret became evident in middle school when he and Alicia were caught naked in her bedroom. What were you doing in that girl's room?" Our mother repeatedly asked to see if Nathan would ever be honest about his behavior.

From that time forward, Nathan admitted his infatuation, but it took a tragic loss of life before he would surrender himself to the infinite mercy who stakes claim on all believers and non-believers. During that time, Nathan got baptized and regularly spent his Sunday mornings attending Bible Study, and regular mass with our grandfather. While Nathan tried keeping his hope about the future on ice, he didn't know a countdown to catastrophe was happening. He started sinking fast when the pivotal point of his life came with brute force on December 2, 2002. This was the day Nathan's quest in an interrogation room would determine his fate forever.

Nathan had turned nineteen-years old a week and five days earlier. In advance of his birthday, he'd returned back to Michigan after being put on leave from his job in Florida. Entertainment was his preferred choice of work with the fortune five hundred company, Walt Disney. As funny, and maybe even as ridiculous as this may sound, Nathan put on a theatrical display around Disney's Parks where literally, he became the whimsical characters we all grew up watching.

When he was accepted into the Disney College Program, the position he originally took was as a gift store manager. He'd always been especially good with sales. Without much consideration, Nathan abandoned his managerial role when recruiters jockeyed for him to become a part of Disney's magical hub of performers. Following a choreographed audition, Nathan took and passed a mandatory class where he studied the history behind most of the Disney characters.

How to display action from within the sweltering costume had to be perfected. Plus, signatures of the animated stars, had to be memorized and executed properly. It was all the test to get Nathan closer to working on one of Disney's cruise ships. Then, when he accomplished the skill to transport himself to the attitude of each character like Disney required, it was time to go to work. MGM Studios, Magic Kingdom, Animal Kingdom, and Epcot all became the platform for where my brother began to melt the hearts of children and adults alike. Nathan was slated to be a part of something so new, so different, and so mysterious.

I suppose he attributes the experience in drama class, taught by his theology teacher at Loyola High School in Detroit, for his acting skills. The standing ovation he once received for playing Flaveus in Julies Caesar gave Nathan the opportunity to perform again amongst a huge crowd in Sarnia, Canada. Thereafter, the Shakespeare play, occasionally he volunteered his craft for other projects associated with Loyola and the catholic church the school was attached with. Excelling academically as well, I remember Loyola holding a ceremony where they inducted Nathan and other classmates into the Honor Society. From then on, his school's basketball team "The Bulldogs," hired him as a team manager. That same year, he helped contribute to the teams' winning of a Catholic Divisional Championship title.

All the people who were closest to my brother, knew his compassion for those who were ill. Throughout his attendance at the all-boys school, Nathan acquired a long lasting friendship with a youngster who suffered from Sickle Cell. With somewhat of a tech style outer appearance, Aden was thin, wore glasses, he was just as short as my brother, and his will despite his illness, was extremely strong. Whenever Aden found himself amongst the cold walls of the place that was supposed to make him better, my brother was the main person from Loyola to always go spend many hours with him. They would talk, laugh, and be creative while the Demerol took effect on his friend.

When they weren't held up by all of Aden's blood transfusions or chronic pains, the two often frequented techno concerts where they always had VIP access. They reveled in the benefit of eating at five star restaurants like the old revolving Summit, the Whitney Mansion, and sometimes even Aden's favorite Japanese restaurant, Bennihannas. Their relationships with staff at their school was so much so that they both were frequently invited to family outings of Loyola's secretaries and teachers. From the outside, it appeared Aden and Nathan were wise beyond their years.

Once Aden was healthy enough to travel, he and Nathan did something they'd talked about doing for a while. Aden wanted to travel to Japan, and Nathan wanted his friend to experience a piece of culture amidst the span of our own country land. Nathan would choose their first line of tours, then their second excursion would be off to the east coast of Asia. With a couple of friends, they packed their bags and started their adventure with a long but wild bus trip down to the southern states. While tomorrow wasn't necessarily promised to either of them, they never got enough of experiencing the world's scenery, culture, food, and Nathan's favorite...the young ladies.

In the weeks following my brother's return from his two week trip, school commenced again. Sooner than we all knew it, a dark cloud hovered over our family the second we learned of our maternal grandmother's departure from this earth. Up until then, we'd never had anyone in our immediate family die on us. It bothered me not to have visited my grandmother the night before, like my mother and Nathan had. Turning out as we hoped though, we sent her off with a fitting funeral, then properly laid her to rest in Plymouth, Michigan.

"I think that woman had something to do with this," my mom on occasion would shout wildly after her mother died.

She was speaking of the woman my grandmother used to tell us she saw roaming around her home at night. For years we figured her visions were embellished a bit. Now that we look at what all transpired after she was gone, her story holds great validity. In fact, Nathan's first arrest was in direct result of the woman who unexpectedly appeared around our grandfather a short time after our grandmother was buried.

Soon after my brother was given news about the mystery woman having took our deceased grandmother's Cadillac, Nathan found out who this person was and where she lived at in the town of Royal Oak. With fierce pleasure he recovered the car from in front of her house with a key he'd been given from our cousin Simon. I have to say, it was a unique approach at what Nathan called an official introduction.

On the day of the car heist, as the sun tucked itself away, my brother called his girlfriend Amelia and asked her to go out to dinner later that evening. She obliged, but only if she could bring a friend. Their tones were filled with so much excitement. After the many years of Amelia and Nathan knowing each other, this was officially going to be their first date out on the town. Nathan first picked up Simon, then Amelia, and together they all headed to downtown Detroit.

The night time sky was clear, and Amelia signaled Nathan to turn towards the lights growing brighter and brighter. Greek Town's restaurant, bars, and casinos were lively with people having a good time. Yet, it was ten or more minutes of waiting in the congested traffic only to make one left turn. Nathan had a sense that maybe the parking area he was driving towards sat too far from where they wanted to eat at. Their direction changed immediately, and the realization that the police were behind them sent Nathan's heart to beat bolistically.

The red and blue lights from the police squad car rapidly strobed through the Cadillac like a rave was going on. When Nathan pulled over, quicker than he seen it coming, the police grabbed ahold of his shirt and pulled him out the car. Everyone inside was hauled over to the infamous 1300 Beaubian Police Headquarters. Inside, my brother saw his girlfriend, the daughter of a city elected judge, sitting behind a desk in an interview room. This was going to be bad if her mom found out, Nathan figured.

Amelia wasn't his adversary, nor did she have anything to do with his decision to take something that did not belong to him. Nathan kept hold of he and Amelia's solidity. After taking full responsibility, my brother was charged with Unlawful use of an Automobile without the Intent to Steal. Months later he was sentenced under a Holmes Youthful Training Act where, once completed, there would be no criminal record.

It came out later that our grandfather's mistress, Lena, forced him to press charges on Nathan. Sadly, we'd also received information from Simon about our mother's father being abused at the hands of Lena. My brother and Simon were enraged. Lena was ten years younger than my mother, with a bad disposition towards everyone in the family. She slowly but surely begun turning the home our grandmother loved so much, into a place that represented her own madness.

She'd went so low as to convince our grandfather to put the vacation home in Oklahoma up for rent, just to stop our family from enjoying the property during the summer months. When that all happened, Nathan narrowed his gaze with what seemed to be retribution. He got so obsessed and out of control with his antics. Nathan started filling out credit card applications in her name. He wrote and cashed checks in her name. There were belligerent messages Nathan would leave on her answering machine. He'd even destroy her expensive furniture or clothes she'd kept at our grandfather's home.

Enough was enough, and in culmination with how Franck was dealing with his eldest son being killed on patrol while acting out his duties as a cop in California, a decision was made for Nathan to go live with his dad. They'd found themselves helping each other with the grieving of Nathan's older brother. My brother's presence was also an opportunity to make up for the lost time that Franck had missed.

The birthplace of jazz had always been Nathan's second home. Franck started work at a ship yard that sat on the wavy Mississippi, while Nathan took on eleventh grade at Sarah T. Reed High School. The school sat in Orleans Parish, in the same district they lived, called New Orleans East. While only there for the period of a year, Amelia kept their bond strong through long phone conversations practically every other night.

The old Spanish style neighborhoods of the French Quarters was periodically a place visited by my brother when he would stay with an aunt who lived uptown. He took pleasure sitting at the historic Café du Monde to eat hot beignets, while listening to old brass bands playing near-by. The sweet tunes always familiarized him with the period of history when he took up both the trombone and tenor saxophone. Unlike the sticking points he couldn't get over with those instruments, swimming was my brother's thing. From the time we learned how to swim during private lessons our mother enrolled us in, and for years before he moved, Nathan swam a bunch. Often, he stroked the waters with us more than anyone else because he always used to say he knew we wouldn't drown him. There were also those times when he and Amelia swam in her grandparents' back yard pool.

New Orleans' famous French Quarters was also a memory of a racial bias situation Nathan and Aden once encountered. Wanting to have lunch at an outside restaurant renowned for playing live music, my brother and his friends sat down at an open table underneath a huge overhang that kept the merciless sun off them. When the waitress came to the table, she appeared nervous. Darting her eyes left, then right, then back at each of them, the waitress' face frowned at the moment of asking whether they could afford to eat there.

When this story was revealed, I was appalled at how a stranger could look at my brother's casual attire and question his ability to pay for anything they offered. Nathan and his friends spoke with the establishments manager about the woman's inelegant words. When the meal was given to them for free, they didn't eat it. They simply left without incident. What a challenge it had to be for all of them to keep their composure because if it were me, I'd probably have ended up creating a scene.

Once Nathan held up his end of the bargain and did well at Sarah T. Reed High School, he returned to Michigan the following summer, suffocating himself with the intimacies Amelia offered. They had a whole lifetime ahead of themselves, and after reuniting there was no rush to do much of anything outside of enjoying their time together. I was observant in those young years then, and I saw my brother's focus on Amelia shifting slowly. It all began when he started going over the Ambassador Bridge and into Canada with his friend Terrell. Windsor, Canada was where by brother met Samantha. She was short, had grey eyes, brunette hair, she was older than Nathan, and her accent stood out. It was somewhat ironic because Amelia and Samantha were similar in appearance. This was not the first time Nathan had ever severed ties with Amelia, and it was a move I know he looks back on and regrets tremendously.

Nathan's concentration was in the right place, but there was not much thought put into some of his actions after he graduated high school. Specifically, when he was younger, he always talked about being either a nuclear physicist or a brain surgeon. When it came to signing up for college, he wanted to major in International Marketing because he enjoyed traveling the world. In search of an actual college to attend, we all waited on responses from each institution Nathan applied to. While our mom gave the impression of wanting him to stay in Michigan, our father wanted Nathan to broaden his horizon some more and go somewhere outside of his comfort zone.

I truly believed my brother was going to leave the state again. When it came time for him to gather all his acceptance letters to make a decision, I'd like to say he took the easy way out. Having received admittance to a total of seven schools outside of the state we lived in, which included my father's alma mater, Alabama State University, Nathan chose to go to a school he visited for forty-five minutes and where the driving distance was forty-five minutes from our house. When I heard he was going to Baker College of Flint, all I could think about was how I was going to have to clean up all the crap he was going to spill when our father kicked him square in the rear.

Nathan got into some pretty reputable colleges. Yet, for some reason he enrolled in classes that anyone off the streets could enroll in. Surprisingly though, our parents didn't showcase any form of disappointment. Nathan went on to live in a dormitory setting where he successfully completed one year of college.

When he was let out for the summer, Nathan accepted a Camp Counselor position with a camp located directly on Higgins Lake in Roscommon, Michigan. While there, high ropes training was an interest of his and he succeeded in getting certified in the specialty. Despite all the hard work he put forth, Nathan never had the chance to put his skill to use with the kids he was responsible for.

It was during the camp's opening ceremony in Detroit when Nathan was escorted to a room in the back of the church. The intentions of the ladies who escorted him seemed to suggest a promotion of some sort, until they said, "we're sorry, but we have to let you go." Our mother's friend, who was a lawyer, demanded a reason for the termination. None was given. So Nathan moved to sue for their breach of his contract.

As the roaring of that situation continued, Nathan found another job at an assembly plant in Farmington, Michigan. They hired him to work on an assembly line that made parts for General Motors. Our mom feared for his safety because she did not want another industrial accident to happen in her family again. Somehow though, Nathan found a way to ease her concerns. Unbeknownst to the automotive parts company though, my brother had already consented to an agreement for work at Disney World. In a matter of weeks, Nathan was going to be saying good-bye to us before he departed for his move to Florida.

Meanwhile, therein lied a desire to find someone who Nathan could grow increasingly crazy about, because Samantha as it turned out, had a struggle mounting within herself. She couldn't stay committed for very long. So...carefully, my brother set off to uncover someone who he felt could handle his work schedule and travels.

It wasn't long before bachelor life for Nathan was over. Her name was Renee, and might I say she was pretty. She had that kind of physical beauty that could make a bar go quiet. Even though I was too young for her at the time, I believed when I got older, she could have become all mine. That would have been the first time I'd ever stole anything from my brother, but it would have been worth it. Renee and Nathan were friends, each-others' confidants, and their love for each other spread like a brush fire in a matter of months of dating.

He loved that girl so much that he drove eighteen hours to Michigan, at her command, and attended a funeral of a person he didn't know just to get an obituary to take back to work, as justification for his absence. Shockingly, at age eighteen to be exact, my brother's intentions with Renee was made clear when he proposed to her at her eighteenth birthday party. Family and friends of Renee looked on with happiness in their eyes and they'd all figured my brother would find himself on one knee. I'm not sure if most seen Nathan proposing before he were to graduate college. What he had not expected was how his pledge to Renee would be tested in so many ways.

First there was Renee's increasing pressure about Nathan's need to stop his association with women he was friends with. Then that turned into a heated incident, in front of her family, where Nathan didn't care for her taking off the engagement ring he worked so hard to buy. At a late night dinner with friends, another altercation ensued when Renee snatched her clasped hand away from Nathan when she saw a guy she knew. Despite their faults, they worked to be better. With all the initiatives they took to solidify the immense love they showcased to each other, Nathan's move to the tourist area of Lake Buena Vista, Florida interfered with the progress they made. While Nathan was still in a state of evolving into complete manhood, when he returned back from Florida, Renee and Nathan moved in together. Shortly after, Nathan put on one of his tailored suits and hooked a position with a marketing company in a matter of days of his return.

Watching Nathan develop into a decorative young man who was full of curiosity and eagerness, has been a life lesson. As assuring as his coming time was, my brother's tide of jubilation was adjourned too early.

There was an emptiness...a big disappointment at those who called themselves friends, but wouldn't stand by my brother's side because they wanted to serve their agenda of getting on television or having their names printed in several newspapers or magazines. Maybe they were all just unfit to deal with a situation like the one Nathan was up against. Whatever the case may have been, my family and I swallowed our pride and looked away from the many who once confided in Nathan.

Even with a form of social pressures to get convictions of suspects that have been painted guilty before trial, Nathan's high dollar attorneys sat down at the gambling table and wagered his life to set forth truth.

4

Demanding Voices

For the person who's only been able to envision what lady liberty looks like in person, I can tell you one thing about her - she's just as massive as the issues our country faces today, tomorrow, and forever. The Bartholi Statute, better known as the Statute of Liberty, is the emblem of America that represents freedom for all. I wonder though, does the infrastructure of prison actually deprive confined men and women of their true liberty?

Personally, as to the manner of construction, I've gathered the most descriptive, yet, demonic snapshots of what the inside and outside of prison physically looks like. My imaginative creations were primarily influenced by movies I'd seen. That was until my mother drove me down Cooper Street in Jackson, Michigan. The look of the town sent a chill up my spine, especially when my sight rested on the housing hub where Nathan was living. My eyes opened wide, and I'd realized the energy of the far stretching brick exterior was like being faced with an earthquake for the first time. The electrons that permeated through my body brought on doses of sharp electrical charges, and I was sure everyone inside had at one time or another experienced the same. Honestly, I was scared, and I was ready to get back on a plane to South Carolina. Emotional is an expression used to explain what my feelings were.

Southern Michigan Correctional Facility, also known as Jackson State Penitentiary, stood five stories high with a succession of small impenetrable windows, one after another. From start to finish, the front of the building looked to be at least a quarter mile long, if not further. More than anything, an illusion can shed light on how physically intimidating the entire place is in person. The warehouse of society's mess-ups was surrounded in tightly staked rustic brown bricks, rows of concrete check points, fences, barbed wire, and armed officers. The prisons' façade gave an appearance of simple frankness for everyone on the road passing by to recognize. It definitely was not a place someone would willingly spend the night at, even if they were afforded some kind of compensation.

A lot was left to be discovered as I built the courage to step out of the car. When I looked far past the parking lot, it was as if I'd began foreseeing Nathan's future if no one garnered support on his behalf. I'd remembered resting my eyes on it when we pulled in, but I couldn't believe my sight. The prison actually had a poorly landscaped cemetery off to the side of the parking lot. It was later I learned that there were no more vacancies for prisoners at that location, but the Department of Corrections did have a much larger burial ground, called Cherry Hill.

As my stride came closer to the sloped entry-way of the prison, I glanced up as if I was looking at a skyscraper. I caught a glimpse of a prisoner looking through a window on the third floor. Breaking the room window out seemed to be an easy way for a prisoner to get free. However, that was unlikely because each square porthole had thick steel covers that prevented a convict from even bothering to attempt such a risky move. Or should I say, the steel covers prevent a person from scaling the walls if they did get past the fortified window.

When we reached the check-in desk inside, I immediately felt the officer's authoritarian vibe. His voice said, "What prisoner are you here to see?" I wanted to use the same emphasis in answering his question, but I was still going to great lengths to adjust to the uncomfortable place I was in. As my mother gave the officer Nathan's name and prisoner number, I thought heavily upon how high of a price misbehavior was costing the men behind all that concrete. The flash point was the price that innocent guys were being forced to pay.

Then I remembered something about the prison. Weeks prior, national news reported about the serious conduct of officials at that specific facility. For instance, a twenty-one year old inmate recently died while in four point restraints and confined in a one-hundred and seven degree segregation cell. A slew of rumors surfaced about the young kid having multiple medical and psychiatric conditions, ultimately placing him at risk of suffering from severe heat related illnesses. Despite the prisoner's condition, he was restrained on a concrete slab with his arms and hands tied down until the moment of his death days later. Reports spread about how he was never seen by a physician or psychiatrist while restrained.

Years later, the Michigan Department of Corrections settled the case for an amount that can't begin to repair the disastrous conduct that took the young kid's life. The notion of us as the public, trusting officers with the handling of our family and friends behind bars...is simply not there. Just look at the deficiencies of the regular police on our streets today. We've witnessed, and continue to experience how police departments in this country cover up illegal behaviors by their personnel.

By the time my mother and I finished checking in at the desk, shift change for the officers was nearing. We'd hoped Nathan would make it to the visiting room quick, so that we wouldn't have to wait until the completion of shift change to see him. At the moment when an assembly of uniformed authorities for the next shift came storming through the front door, we anxiously raised from our seats when our names were called. A short-haired officer, wearing a neatly pressed short sleeve, gray shirt, with black pants, gestured for my mother and I to step towards a thick glass-paned sliding door. The entry point was controlled by someone in a station we couldn't see. Once we went through the door, everything past that point evoked mystery to me, and it brought on a bit of nervousness.

Momentarily, we were between two security doors and it was as if they'd made sure you stood there watching all the TV monitors that were on display. The clarity of all the video feed would definitely deter people from smuggling anything in or out of the place. Next, our bodies had to pass a thorough pat down before we walked through a metal detector. It was all a horse and pony show to me. It seemed like the bulk of the contraband the Department of Corrections didn't want getting in, the staff themselves were probably the culprits for a percentage of it getting into prisoners' hands.

At the end of the airport style security, we were welcomed by the grandeur of the vaulted, rotunda shaped, visiting room. It sort of reminds one of the section in the United States Capitol that houses historical art and statues. Like the suction from a vacuum, we met Nathan with warm embraces while our eyes welled up with tears. This was the nearest we'd been in years. I had now grown taller than him. The southern sun had made me much darker than him, and indeed my sense of style of dress had grown much like his once was.

"How do you like the place?" Nathan asked me in a jokingly manner.

I finished wiping the tears off my face, then slightly chuckled to keep from crying any more. "The only thing I have good to say about this dungeon is that you've got top-notch security."

Before our mother went into her nurturing mode, we were given instructions on where to sit. Shortly after taking our seats our mother asked, "Do either of you want something to eat?"

As a small touch of normalcy and comfort, the visiting area provided a selection of vending machines with a variety of microwaveable foods, candies, ice cream and sodas. At her return from getting something for us all to snack on, Nathan and I were already embedded in a conversation about the poor quality foods they gave him, the situations he'd witnessed, and most importantly we quickly ran through how he was spending his time. Beyond all that, my mother and I pointed out everything going on with the entire family. The remarkable part of that day was, after a while, it did not seem like we were in a prison setting.

When the energy of our discussions seemed to begin dying down, I seized the opportunity to start a conversation about the day of his arrest. I scooted my chair more along the front of Nathan, then looked him in his brown eyes.

"You have to trust my attitude with helping you out of this mess."

"That's too big of a commitment for a high schooler, isn't it?"

"Come on Nathan...I need you to be serious."

"Fine! You want me to be honest," Nathan said sternly.

As soon as I opened my mouth to respond, he quickly interrupted me.

"You're not a criminal attorney Axel. So what can you accomplish that I can't?"

"For starters, I have my freedom. That means I have endless connections to people and information that you don't have."

"So you mean to tell me you have these so called people at your disposal at the same time you're living off an allowance."

After Nathan said what was on his mind, it was like an early Sunday morning in church. I shook my head in disbelief. Nathan wasn't looking at the big picture. Why was he being so stubborn? I was trying to be the catalyst that helped bring his freedom back, but he was letting my age consume his feelings.

Like most older brothers, Nathan was one to always help me and teach me. He was a brother who would always listen. I could always count on him. He didn't judge anyone, and he always made me laugh. Now though, he was being a pain in my side, and I quickly expressed my issues about him, to him. Our mother interjected in the conversation and told my brother to listen to what I was trying to convey to him. The difference this time was, he could no longer interrupt me.

Nevertheless, when my last thought escaped me, my mother remarked, "This is like what happens in the courtroom." She shared with us this idea about working together instead of talking over one another. My brother tried cutting her off, but she resisted his statement and cut back in, "Nathan!" She said authoritatively, "You're going to sit here and give your brother the facts of those police reports."

"Why can't I just mail them to Axel so he can see it for himself?"

"Because I brought him here so he can get it out your own mouth."

Nathan gave a bit of an objective look at our mom. I believed in that moment I had uncovered why my brother was being so standoffish, and it wasn't because our mother was there. Not only did I believe it was upsetting for him to re-live that particular day, but he feared shutting down because of how deeply rooted the victim was in our family.

After a momentary mental freeze, Nathan took down his line of defense and began expelling the information he kept locked away in his isolation box.

5

Mayhem

Winters in Michigan are cold...but the weather at the beginning of the season reminds me of how close Christmas is. It was December 2, 2002 when the wind, in the city of Southfield, was rubbing its' invisible body through the branches of all the trees. The temperature outside stood steady in the high single digits, and the roads were being drizzled with sleet. The entwined streets of the rich suburban community called "The Ravines," began getting slushy, while the uniformed men in blue kept encircling the neighborhood in their patrol cars. Ten minutes prior, a call from detectives at Lathrup Village Police Department, was the reason why the morning calm was shattered.

"911, what's the address of your emergency?"

With hysteria, the caller screamed to the dispatcher, "You guys need to get here, there's a lady at our bank who's been a victim of an attempted robbery."

"What's the location of your bank ma'am?"

"We're in Lathrup Village right on Ten Mile."

"Is the victim injured?"

"I don't think so."

"Does anyone know how many suspects there are or who the robbers may be?"

"Not to my knowledge."

"Can you describe the clothing the suspects are wearing?"

"I'm not sure of all that either."

"Do you know if they are armed?"

"The woman was yelling they were."

"Did anyone see what direction the suspects may have went?"

"No, I'm sorry...No, I don't know."

Minutes before, a woman walked into Bank One with loose snow falling from the sleeves of her long, brown, wool coat. She had a phone pressed to her ear, and her direction inside focused on the bank slips that sat to the right of the entry way. When she picked up a withdrawal form, her alarming, boisterous out cry suddenly startled everyone inside.

"I need the police, I've been robbed and ran over."

Within a short space of time, following the bank manager's call to police, Lathrup Village Police Department met with the woman at the center of the purported crime who had allegedly been the victim.

"Ma'am tell us what's going on," a uniformed officer told her.

She identified herself as Lena Rodgers to the first investigator. The original incident occurred in Southfield, she told police.

"I loaned my Jeep to my friend, Sharon Whitehead, so she could take Mr. Harrell to the store."

When she paused, one of the officers who was busy taking notes, intervened and asked, "Who is Mr. Harrell?"

Lena revealed that her and Sharon were both caregivers to my grandfather, at his home in the City of Southfield. Sharon unexpectedly showed up at Lena's home in Royal Oak, honking the horn in a hasty state. When Lena went out into the blistering weather to see what Sharon wanted, Sharon told her that my grandfather wasn't answering his phone.

Once the two women arrived at my grandfather's residence, Lena says she went to the front entrance while Sharon went to a side door. Sharon entered the attached garage, but then came back out approximately thirty seconds later, and just stood by the door. The lead officer asked about whether my grandfather's not answering his phone has ever happened before.

"Yes, it's occurred a few times," Lena mentioned.

"In those instances, was he in need of any kind of aid or medical assistance?"

"Uh...no, I don't believe so."

"Okay, so can you get to the robbery."

Reaching a key inside the keyhole to gain entry, Lena contended Nathan opened one of the double doors, pulled her by the coat, then dragged her inside the house. At that time, Lena described how Nathan sprayed her with a can of Raid and shoved her to the ground.

"I thought I was going to die," she said to the officers in a tone that seemed uncertain.

"Why do you say that?" An officer asked.

"He put a plastic bag over my head while he jabbed me with a butter knife."

"Who's he?"

"Nathan did."

Bringing attention to the minor injuries on her left hand, an officer asked, "I take it that's why your hand is bleeding?"

"I grabbed the knife in an attempt to get the thing away."

"So what happened next?" the officer asked.

"I saw a silver automatic handgun he had stuffed in his waistband. Nathan pointed it at me and told me to walk towards the master bedroom."

"What happened when you went into the room?"

Lena gave her account to authorities as to how she saw her patient, my grandfather, sitting in a chair tied up with tape over his mouth.

"Mr. Harrell was alive and he was so scared," she emphasized.

The second suspect, Lena admitted, was my cousin Simon.

"Simon was holding Nicolas prisoner at gun point," Lena cried out.

According to her version of events, Nathan told Lena to gather all of our grandfather's check books and other miscellaneous items from an adjacent office.

"Were there any other suspects?"

"After Nathan forced me out the front door so we could go to the bank, I saw Simon and Nathan's friend. They call him Ethan?"

"You know his last name?"

"Burton I believe."

"What was Ethan's role?"

"He was sitting in the white Mercedes parked in the driveway by the bushes of the exit gate."

"Was the car there when you and Sharon pulled up?"

"I can't say if it was or wasn't because no one can see that side of the driveway when you first enter the property. The trees obstruct your view."

Continuing on, Lena described how Sharon was already in the rear seat of the Jeep when her and Nathan stepped in to drive off to a nearby bank.

"Nathan first drove to the Mobil gas station up the hill on 9 Mile, and then went inside to pay for gas."

"How long was he gone?"

"About three or four minutes. Something like that."

"During the time Nathan was in the gas station, why didn't you and Sharon just run away?" The reporting officer asked inquisitively.

"I couldn't! I felt like Sharon was involved because Nathan never tried restraining her."

"So when you arrived here at this bank, what happened?"

"I went in while Sharon and Nathan stayed in the car."

Once inside, Lena indicated she grabbed a withdrawal slip then went back outside and told Nathan she couldn't get any money out of the bank. When she went back to the Jeep, Lena mentioned how it was strange that Sharon was standing outside in the cold, looking at her through the window with crazy eyes. In an attempt to grab her keys out of the ignition, while the passenger side door was open, Lena explained how Nathan put the car in reverse. This caused her to fall out of the passenger side door and onto the ground.

"He ran me over with my truck," she screamed out.

In her last recount of events, officers were told about how Nathan left the scene in her Jeep while Sharon left either on foot or possibly in the Mercedes driven by Ethan. While Lena's account was being recorded by Lathrup Village Police, the Southfield Police Department was contacted and dispatched to my grandfather's house on Timberline Drive in Southfield.

Prior to entering my grandfather's home, officers were briefed about Simon allegedly holding our grandfather captive. Seconds before the call came out over the bull-horn for those inside to come out with their hands up, it was broadcasted over the radio that Nathan was being pursued in a high speed chase down a main road somewhere in Southfield.

Meanwhile, a group of officers entered the home through an unlocked door. After an initial search of the entire place, they found no one. They called more officers and did a second sweep. Still, they found no one. It wasn't until a third look through the house when a shout from the master bedroom rung out.

"I think we've got something in here."

Two burly officers hurried to their comrades echoing words.

"We need to lift this up, it's something back there."

As the officers took to the corners of the made up bed, they raised the mattress and box spring, then sat it against the long dresser to the back of them. The clearance underneath the bed was entirely too tight for anyone to hide, but there was an hidden spot in the middle of the armoire style cabinets on each side of the headboard, where they found the body of my grandfather.

Upon issuance of a warrant authorizing a search of the home, financial documents, bills, and other correspondences were recovered before the scene was turned over to Southfield Forensics Crime Lab specialists. A short time after the crime lab took control of the scene, Simon and Ethan were arrested, at Ethan's parents' home, about a mile from my grandfather's.

Succeeding one of Lena's interviews with a veteran investigator for the Southfield Police Department, she sat in Providence Hospital Emergency Room and wrote a statement clarifying her claims. At the end of her tell-all, she concluded the interview with a strong statement.

"Those boys killed him." When the detective asked who, Lena responded, "Nathan, Simon, and Ethan." Though there were no obvious signs of death, and since the autopsy was not concluded until the following day, it raised officers' eyebrows when Lena expressed knowing that my grandfather had been killed.

I must confess, as I sat there listening to my brother and mother explain the grim sequence of events which the police reports back up, I was desperate for answers about why Simon and Ethan were never held accountable. I was also eager to hear about the story surrounding his car chase.

"Why did you speed away from the police?" I asked Nathan.

"How do you explain a lapse in judgment?" he started off saying. Nathan tried being more thoughtful and intentional with what my ears heard, but I told him simply, "Just be honest with me."

He'd brought attention on how jail was a sure thing.

"Why?" our mother blurted out.

Nathan took a breath and said he'd done some things that he couldn't fix.

"Like what?" I jumped in to ask.

It would take another round of going back and forth with two word questions and answers before Nathan admitted to being worried about the physical altercation he and Lena found themselves in. Regardless of the consequences for the assault, there was still the issue of him attempting to bleed her dry of money she shared with our grandfather.

Nathan wanted to position himself to know everything Lena and our grandfather were doing. In fact, when Lena offered my brother a position at her Boutique, Nathan grabbed the opportunity. Lena's connection with my grandfather reeked so much havoc on Nathan that it changed the quality of his existence. Nathan disliked her so much, he figured getting close to Lena was his ticket. There was a time when Nathan falsely lead Lena to believe that his time at her Boutique could lead to a future in which they would develop a better relationship. Consequently, after a disagreement over time helping at the shop, suspicion arose about Nathan's actual motives regarding their relationship. This ended up with him being terminated.

Afterwards, Nathan fell back to his crutch, and his antics became more brash. Before long, there were instances where Nathan became the number one suspect for credit card scams, forgery, theft of cash, and receiving stolen merchandise. He'd took his addiction out on Lena, other family members, friends, and people he didn't know. I also didn't know if Nathan felt owed something from others, or whether it was a matter of him making bad choices. His struggle with taking things that didn't belong to him had its' ups and downs. The reality was, Nathan did not need for a single thing on this earth. In terms of him simply wanting to have something, well, he'd always been urged to work, but he could have asked and received anything from anyone in our family, but he chose to be a kleptomaniac.

Simon and Nathan set the tone of working together when they were in middle school and would steal large bundles of cash that our grandparents would have hidden. They would get caught stealing from stores, while having in their pockets hundreds of dollars they'd stolen. Then, the problem escalated to stealing expensive cars despite both having one of their own. Luckily, our parents or grandparents would bail them out so that jail didn't become their destiny.

"So when you left Lena at the bank, what were you going to do with her car?" I asked.

Nathan's silence came off as if he was beginning to feed me a lie.

"The only thing we have control of," Nathan said, then continued, "are the decisions we invite in our lives."

"That doesn't answer my question."

"I'd figured she made her decision of messing up everything since grandma died. So I was going to destroy her car."

The truth was, I figured, Nathan had no plan. He'd landed at the bottom by the time he got into his troubles that day, and the waves were drifting him in hazardous directions.

"So how did you end up in police custody?"

"I was driving down 9 Mile where a police car scanned Lena's license plate. When the police got behind me I punched the gas and tried running away from them."

"How fast were you going?"

"I don't know! Somewhere around ninety miles, maybe close to a hundred miles per hour."

"On the slippery roads?" I asked with absolute shock.

"Up until the time I came over the hill and crashed into a car waiting at the light."

Nathan wanted to reassure me no one got hurt in the crash.

"After I hit the car, I got out and ran across Lasher Road, which is where I was cornered and arrested."

When I interrupted Nathan from moving ahead in his flashback, my face gave my mother and him a curious expression before asking, "Simon and Ethan, why weren't they charged?"

Nathan shook his head in a negative motion when our mother responded, "They both took and passed polygraphs."

"That's how they were able to be released from any of the charges," Nathan said.

"Why didn't you take a polygraph?"

"They never came to me about one."

"Wait a minute!" I turned toward my mother and uncrossed my legs. "I'm not understanding this," I paused to collect my thoughts, then continued. "But, how did Simon pass a polygraph if he was the one in the room with grandad?"

Nathan looked at me in my eyes and said, "I'll tell you like I was trying to tell the police from the beginning. They were not there!"

"So Lena told them a lie?"

"Of course! And remember her telling the police how grandad was tied and taped up?"

The anticipation of what I was about to say suddenly lingered with silence as I tried putting my words together. My mother cut in and spoke the answer to what my mind was about to tell my lips to ask.

"Neither of those assertions are true Axel. The autopsy and forensic report found no evidence of your grandfather being tied or taped up in any fashion. They didn't even find a single strand of twine or duct tape in the entire damn house."

"Were there other untruths Lena told the detectives or police?" I asked eagerly.

"Remember Sharon Whitehead?" Nathan asked.

"Yeah! Where did they find her at?"

"Turned out she was fictitious, so Lena claimed," my mother said with a disappointing look.

I leaned forward a short ways and tucked my face into my hands with astonishment. Everything I was hearing sounded unreal. It was all bizarre, and I was beginning to be aggressively concerned with why Lena wasn't in prison.

"You mean to tell me Lena made this Sharon woman up too?" I muttered while separating my head from the clasp position it was in.

"That's what she testified to," my mother answered.

Personally, I can't say with conviction that I believe Lena deserved physical retribution for all the disturbances she'd created for our family and Ethan's family. However, I was convinced by what I was hearing that she knew more than what detectives were being lead to believe. I'd thought in those moments of how if I was an officer in charge that day, I would have treated her like the military does terrorists.

"Anything else I should know about?"

"Well, they never found whatever gun she said Nathan had. And during your brother's trial, Lena couldn't even remember telling the police he even had a gun."

The poison Lena kept spreading did not end with the police. She brought her theatrics into the courtroom too. In the presence of the jury, Nathan's attorneys asked what her and my grandfather's relationship was.

"We were friends," Lena answered.

"Were you his caregiver?"

Lena steadfastly said, "No...the media got it wrong. He was my caregiver."

"Could you explain what you mean by that?"

"A caregiver is someone that takes me shopping. He was also the conservator over all my money."

"So he took you shopping?"

"Yes!"

"For things like what?"

"All types of things."

"Did you have a Saks charge card in Mr. Harrell's name?"

"I don't believe so."

"You don't believe you did?"

"I was an authorized user."

It was worth putting a period on Lena's sentence so that the jury could be reminded about how she was allegedly run over. With a strong appetite to nail her, my brother explained how one of his fierce approaching attorneys continued on.

"Were you rolled over by the tires of your SUV?"

Lena responded with a definite, "Yes!"

"Who's name is on that vehicle?"

"Both me and Mr. Harrell's."

"What other vehicles do you own with Mr. Harrell?"

"A Chrysler 300, a Lincoln Town Car, a Saab, a Mercedes car and a Mercedes truck."

"How many of those cars are kept at Mr. Harrell's home in Southfield?"

"None!"

"Is it correct that he can fit four cars in his garage on Timberline and maybe twenty more in his driveway?"

"I don't know about twenty, but maybe."

"Are all those vehicles at your home?"

"Not all of them, but most."

"Ms. Rodgers, did you suffer any fractures after being ran over?"

"No!"

"Any bruises?"

"No!"

"But, Ms. Rodgers you said your legs were rolled over."

Nathan found nothing to be hysterical as he was fighting for his life, but members of the audience uncontrollably laughed out loud at Lena's testimony. Judge McDonald, who was known for his calm temper, immediately halted the proceedings and cut in, "Excuse me...You guys keep laughing and you're out of here. This isn't funny! I don't care what you're laughing about, stop it!"

After the aggressive hammer was sat down, Lena's phone call in the bank was brought forward.

"Before you told the bank to call 911, you were on the phone correct?" Nathan's attorney asked.

"No. I was not on the cellphone as I walked in the bank."

"If there was evidence that was presented that said you were on a cellphone per bank video, that evidence would be wrong?"

"I mean, I was on my cellphone telling someone to go to my home."

"And who were you talking to?"

"A friend."

"What's their name?"

"Brian Tally."

"And Mr. Tally was staying with you after being dishonorably discharged from the military, is that correct?"

"Yes!"

"Ms. Rodgers, you'd just been, as you described, almost killed, but you yourself didn't call 911?"

"No, I did not."

Next, Nathan and my mother described to me how his attorney asked Lena if she had a revelation about my grandfather being killed.

"The detectives misunderstood my statement," Lena said.

"But Ms. Rodgers, the police reports are clear and it reflects precisely what you told them, is that right."

Just as Nathan's attorney waited for Lena's response, her statement was pulled from a folder to recollect her memory in the manner she denied making such a remark. Instead of answering the question, she remained silent. Her appearance looked as if she genuinely was not sorry for her actions, my mother explained.

"Ms. Rodgers, what address was on your identification when this incident happened?"

"The address on Timberline Drive."

"That's where Mr. Harrell was found, correct?"

"Yes!"

"Would you mind telling the court how many other homes you own with Mr. Harrell?"

"There's a total of four other ones."

"What cities are they in?"

"Birmingham, Walled Lake, Royal Oak and Farmington Hills."

PDF 87

When asked about whether she would have voluntarily went into the police department to say she lied on innocent people, Lena's response was a bit shaky.

"I called the police back when they asked me to."

"No dear, that's not voluntarily righting your wrongs," one of Nathan's attorneys commented.

The power of an apology for some individuals is priceless. Lena, however, didn't seem to have that in her because she'd never confronted her indiscretions with Simon or Ethan when they were released.

It was eight days later when detectives told Lena her details were incorrect. She then testified that her story changed after detectives called her back to the police station.

"Ms. Rodgers, was your name on the house the police found Mr. Harrell at?"

She seemed dumbfounded about how to answer. It took Nathan's attorney three times to ask the question in varying ways in order for her to get around to saying, "Yes!"

"So you and Mr. Harrell have five homes together?"

"Yes!"

"Did you tell anyone you and Mr. Harrell had plans to marry?"

"He may have told one of our neighbors we were because the neighbor mentioned it to me. But I don't remember if I did."

"How many names did you go by?"

"Just one."

"So when investigators testified that you gave them three different names, are they wrong?"

"I gave them my married name and two other names. So yeah, that would be correct."

"Why were you switching your name with each investigator you spoke with?"

"I don't really know."

"Okay, Ms. Rodgers, when you told dispatch that somebody had taken your car, why does it reflect that you didn't immediately give them Nathan's name?"

"I was upset. I gave them a description of him being a little boy. I couldn't think of his name."

"How long have you known Mr. Harrell?"

"About five years."

"And you know Nathan at sight right?"

"Yes!"

What was striking was how I wasn't hearing a single thing to indicate how Nathan was responsible for anything monstrous. For sure, there was a scarcity of applying justice to the one individual who was ravaged with blatant lies and cover-ups. My opinion however, differed from what the court system and police apparently deemed correct. I didn't want to become a bit accusatory and say to my brother, "You were at the house when grandad got killed." So I set off to build a line of communication around the forensics collected at the scene.

"Forensics was clear cut," my mother said.

The crime scene investigation personnel collected:

> ☒ Eleven fingerprint lifts
> ☒ Acrylic Fingernails
> ☒ A bloody pillow case
> ☒ A sponge in the master bedroom that had blood stains on it
> ☒ The comforter that was on my grandfathers bed
> ☒ Swabs of blood from the master bedroom floor
> ☒ Swabs of blood from the on-suite master bathroom sink basin, rim, and facet handle
> ☒ Blood stains from a checkbook register
> ☒ Blood stains next to a phone stand in a hallway
> ☒ The clothing my grandfather was wearing when police found him, and;
> ☒ Fingernail clippings of my grandfather

"What were the results of all that stuff?" I asked Nathan and my mother.

"None of the fingerprints were Nathan's," my mother said while continuing. "None of the blood was Nathan's. The blood stained comforter was never tested. The blood in the hallway never got tested. And Lena's blood was found to be positive on the master bedroom floor and bathroom sink," my mother explained.

"The coroner said there was an apparent struggle, but the lead detective never submitted the fingernail clippings to be tested," Nathan admitted.

I flashed a look that seemed to say, what were the detectives thinking. My mother's face registered a bit confusing as well, and then she said, "Tell your brother what Lena said about her blood getting into areas of the house."

"Let me guess," I paused, then grinned slightly. "She said the testing was wrong, and that it wasn't her blood, right?"

Nathan's trial took a dramatic turn when his attorneys hurriedly approached Lena with the question of her DNA being found near my grandfather's body.

"I don't know how my blood came to be in the master bedroom because I never went in there," Lena answered assuredly.

There was one thing out of all others that stood out about her answer. Everyone in the court room knew she was lying. Without giving a second opportunity to change her story, Nathan's attorney needed for her to corroborate a piece of evidence that seemed so obvious. Lena was asked, "Ms. Rodgers, tell us the truth. Were you stabbed? Because the crime scene investigators never found a knife with blood on it."

"I wasn't stabbed, and I don't know where the blood came from," Lena told the court.

Just as Nathan started to open up, a correctional officer came around telling the families in the visiting room they had five more minutes until visits ended for the day. I couldn't believe how time flew by so quick. So before my mother and I set off, I wanted to fill in another missing piece to the puzzle.

"Since there were no obvious signs of how grandad died, what was the actual cause of death?"

"The Chief Medical Examiner said it was asphyxia due to oxygen deprivation. The doctor couldn't be specific as to how the injuries came about, but he said something physical had to have happened."

"Is there more than one way for someone to be asphyxiated?"

"They said there's many ways. Some more obvious than others."

"Did they find out about what time he may have died?"

"The time of death was ruled to be unknown."

"How do they not come up with a time of death," I said with a roaring tone.

The days of sadness consuming my life was long gone, but it was disheartening to see my brother in prison where the bulk of the state's case pointed in another direction. It pained my family and I to fly down life's path without my big brother as our co-pilot. It's even more unsteady in our journey knowing my mother's father had not received a more scrutinizing investigation into his murder.

How was my brother convicted on such weak evidence? I found it incredibly difficult to believe what I was made abreast of was the end all be all to Nathan's case. There had to be things that put Nathan on the police's radar because I'd remembered parts of those conversations our dad used to have with Nathan over the phone. I was sure my visit with Nathan the next day would probably be spent nodding my head with displeasure at the facts of the ever evolving story.

6

Reflections

Throughout the time I sat by the window in the hotel suite my mother and I stayed at overnight, flashes of Nathan's life amongst the squalid prison environment manifested into other concentrations. While the television was busy developing the nightly programs and such, the screen was pretty much watching me look out at the stars. I soaked in the interesting reflections of the infinite universe, and I wondered about my grandfather's spirit inhabiting the expansive heavens.

Memories of the songs my grandfather practiced over and over at home, is a constant reminder of how faithful he was to the church he was a member of for over twenty-years. In fact, as Deacon for St. Paul Tabernacle in Detroit, he had a profound effect on lots of kids within the church. My grandfather's wisdom wasn't limited to just those youngsters though. Not long after our grandmother died from complications of a brain surgery, my grandfather filled Nathan's heart with the encouragement to finally get baptized and join St. Paul Tabernacle. My brother's primary goal to surrender over to God had been reached and his overwhelming convictions, on occasion, stood on the brink of getting wadded-up and thrown in a wastebasket when Lena influenced our grandfather to press charges on him once more.

The south side of Chicago was where my grandfather escaped from after graduating high school. So he used to say, he'd shoved all the photographic memories he had during war in a corner, then came back to America and married my grandmother. Traveling the world throughout most of their lives, they left remnants of their love everywhere they went. Pictures and stories from family serve as a great part of my recollection of both my maternal grandparents. What jogged my brain amidst most of these news worthy stories I heard growing-up were the accounts about my grandfather's uncanny relationship with Lena.

"What are you thinking about?" my mother asked when she sat in the armchair to the right of me.

"I can't believe how that woman had the gull to say all those lies, yet not raise any red flags."

"There's a lot of other issues dealing with that woman that wasn't brought up in your brother's trial."

"Let me guess, she's been in trouble with the law once before."

My mother said further, "when both my sisters moved back to Michigan and lived over at your grandfather's, Lena would come over when they weren't there and steal some of your aunts' belongings. She also went so far as to put locks on the bedrooms they were staying in. And when I would call on occasion, the crazy woman would cuss me out and tell me not to bother with calling my father. Nor did she want any of us visiting him."

"Did you tell the police about any of that?"

"I told them she contacted us the day after your grandfather's death and said the family had no right to his things."

"What about Lena putting a personal protection order on Simon's girlfriend? Did you let detectives know of that?"

"No, I just figured they would find out most of what they needed to know from my sisters, since those two were the ones who had the most dealings with your grandfather's girlfriend."

With all due respect to my mother and her siblings, I silently wondered throughout our open discussion how it was they'd let this stranger infiltrate our family. It all goes back to the words of my grandmother when she was living. She tried warning us about there being a woman the entire time lurking around her home in the night hours. My question of why no one stepped in to make sure my grandfather was competent enough to make decisions, haunted my shuteye for a great part of the darkened hours.

7

Waiving Away Safeguards

C oming after the rise of the sun which gave us all light
that following morning, my mother and I prepared to
go see Nathan a final time before we left Michigan. Finally,
I thought, the absence of details which left a tremendous
void in my understanding about the complexity of Nathan's
conviction, was soon to mature into existence. Would what he
was gearing up to tell me alter my interest in his conviction? I
know that truth isn't always easy to find. Nonetheless, I would
be largely insulted if he didn't tell me what the true facts were.

At first glance into my brother's eyes, he looked at me
with such deep respect when he placed several thick manila
envelopes onto the small coffee table in front of us.

"In case I miss something here, all the information you
need is in this package."

"What does it have in it?" I asked with an obvious restless
eagerness.

"Copies of police reports, transcripts, briefs and opinions
from the court."

At the moment when I was getting ready to add to the
conversation, my brother raced to ask me what my opinions

on uninformed suspects were. It was a topic I brought up in the letter to him prior to my visit, but I never touched base on how I felt with regards to the issue. While I went on unraveling what was forefront on my mind, Nathan veered in between my statement and told me to listen closely to something he wanted me to translate. Suddenly, he started reciting the familiar words I was used to hearing from all types of cop shows.

You have the right to remain silent. Anything you say can be used against you in a court of law. You have the right to talk to a lawyer and have him present with you while you are being questioned. If you cannot afford to have a lawyer, one will be appointed to represent you before any questioning. If you decide to answer questions now without a lawyer present, you will still have the right to stop answering at any time until you talk to a lawyer.

Not of my own doing, but the energy from the annunciation of those words had me feeling like I was on the edge of a precipice. It felt like the wind was going to tip me over into some serious trouble. The power of those words alone are indicative of someone being questioned. The importance of those minimal phrases is supposed to protect all Americans from the punishing crawl of using what you say in a court of law. The question remains though, how many teens and how many young adults actually understand the requirement to carefully consider those rights? Do they know the complexity of how those rights apply in situations when they're being questioned or investigated for a crime with which they may or may not have committed? If one were to waive those rights for whatever reason, are the youth of today informed of those dangers from doing so?

"Do you have any ideas what those rights are called?" Nathan asked me as if he was my teacher.

"Not off the top of my head."

"Miranda Rights!" That's what it's called. They were adopted by the United States Constitution's Fifth Amendment. It was set in place to protect you from self-incrimination, and provide you with due process of law, and fair treatment during investigations."

"Okay, so explain to me exactly how self-incrimination, due process of law and fair treatment ties in with your case."

"It all started after I made the wrong decision to waive my rights."

"How does a person waive their rights?

"When you're arrested and interrogated by the police, they are to give you a recital of your rights."

"Okay!"

"You have an option to say you waive these rights, which gives them authority to ask you questions. Or, you can tell them you're not waiving your rights, and that you want an attorney before speaking to them."

"Which is better?"

"Don't ever waive your right to remain silent until you're able to speak with an attorney," Nathan said absolutely.

"Why? What if I didn't do anything wrong and they wanted to talk to me about a particular situation I knew answers to?"

In response to Nathan foregoing his Miranda Rights following his arrest, he went on to explain how detectives first put him in a narrow, windowless room that was occupied with a small table and two chairs. After my brother's body was examined for signs and marks indicative of a struggle, detectives determined nothing was visible. Nathan put on a jail uniform after his clothing was collected, then the detectives bound him down with shackles and handcuffed his wrist to a metal ring attached to the wall. He was soon to find out that the first interrogation of his life was going to be like a snowball coming down a hill. The chaos that would ensue was going to get bigger, even bigger, then humongous.

The lead investigator was Detective Dan Rizzuto, a thin Italian fellow with a long face, wide nose, and a full head of shiny, slicked back hair. At first appearance he looked to be a man who absolutely wished he had a different profession. As an officer of the law, Rizzuto had a little over five years with the Los Angeles Police Department, two years with the Ann Arbor Police Department in Michigan, nine years with the Southfield Police Department and only seven of those years had been spent on assignment as a detective.

The day my grandfather was found, Rizzuto was working with a team of four other detectives who deal with miscellaneous crimes in the city of Southfield. In a secondary role, Rizzuto had the assistance of a six foot, African American detective, whose name was William Summers. Their first line of business was to ascertain my brother's involvement based upon the preliminary information they'd gathered from Lena. While the status of the investigation was still a bit limited to Rizzuto and Summers, they'd known about my grandfather being found deceased in his home. Neither detective said anything to Nathan about the death. Although they weren't required to mention the crisis, they told my brother there was an incident and they wanted clarification as to what transpired.

As Nathan's adrenaline subsided, his hip started to throb with pain as he gave both detectives details about what he'd done. At the initiation of his account, detectives were made aware of Nathan's injury that stemmed from the crash that happened thirty-minutes earlier. However, both investigators were persistent on moving the investigation forward.

"Let me tell you what I know," Detective Rizzuto said, looking at Nathan with his stern eyes from across the table.

"What you tell us now will effect your future if we don't get the truth."

Over the next couple of hours Nathan dove directly into his first statement. He started off explaining how our grandfather woke him up and said he needed to leave because his girlfriend was coming over. Making the decision to stay a while longer, Nathan's written statement talked about how Lena came to the home and immediately went inside our grandfather's room after entering the front door. After approximately twenty minutes of being in the master suite, she comes back to the front of the house where her and my brother made visual contact inside the kitchen. A confrontation ensued where Nathan sprayed Lena with an insecticide in her eyes. While questions of her profiting handsomely was brought to the forefront of their squabble, Lena offered my brother one-hundred thousand dollars to right whatever wrongs she felt Nathan thought she was responsible for.

As calm settled over the kitchen, Nathan detailed how Lena grabbed an envelope from one of the kitchen counters and handed it to him. Until the time they were in the car going to a bank, where Lena convinced my brother to believe she was going to give back some of what she took from our grandfather, Nathan told detectives that he didn't understand how it was she kept bleeding. Then strangely, Nathan tells the police, Lena started talking about how she admired Nathan for going to college and working, but she couldn't stand what Simon was doing with himself.

"It seemed like she was working an angle of some kind," Nathan utters to detectives before moving forward. "And I couldn't put my finger on what that was."

Arriving at Bank One in Lathrup Village, Nathan ended up leaving the bank parking lot and quickly headed back to Southfield to retrieve some of his belongings. As the sounds of police sirens neared our grandfather's home, Nathan revealed that he left without speaking to our grandfather because he didn't see him. A short time later, Nathan admitted to panicking as he sped away from police.

The first interrogation started at 2:30p.m. and ended at 5:50. It was followed by an additional question and answer which was completed at 6:05.

Developments from the varying officers interviewing Lena, seemed to be inconsistent with what Nathan had already told Rizzuto and Summers. Detectives were positive other individuals were involved, and they wanted to know why Nathan hadn't implicated those who Lena said were a part of the robbery and kidnapping, including her friend Sharon Whitehead.

At around a quarter to 7:00 the night of Nathan's first interrogation, Rizzuto and Summers congregated around Nathan, who was still harnessed to the wall, and they'd mentioned a number of charges he was facing. To keep from being indicted on kidnapping, felonious assault, robbery, fleeing and eluding and grand-theft of a motor vehicle, Nathan was told he needed to corroborate what the police were already aware of. Rizzuto and Summers wanted Nathan to re-evaluate his stance on protecting anyone involved.

"Simon and Ethan were not there. I'm telling you she's lying."

Detectives didn't like my brother vehemently denying their false assertions. With Rizzuto's level of anger spilling forth, he admitted in court testimony that the trajectory of his tone was dependent upon Nathan's statements not adding up to what he and his investigators wanted to hear. Another piece that was missing, Detective Rizzuto testified to in regards to Nathan's second interview, "Nathan made no mention about his grandfather being deceased at the scene."

When one of my brother's attorneys asked Rizzuto about the snippets of information he and Summers said they informed Nathan of during this second interrogation, Rizzuto said, "I can't remember what I told him because I didn't notate anything about what I said."

Continuously hammering Nathan with information about other individuals being involved, a second statement encompassing the names Lena and the police swore were culpable, was added to my brother's second verbal and written statement.

"So you told Nathan something, and then he gave you a statement that included what you said," Nathan's attorney asked Detective Rizzuto.

"True, in a sense," Rizzuto answered.

Ending the barrage of arduous police tactics by nine that night, detectives were encouraged to have broken my brother's will. The law officials had drained Nathan by keeping him secured to a wall, they got in his face and shouted at him, they didn't give him medical treatment right away, and they scared him into believing he was facing a bunch of felony charges. All along, Detective Rizzuto's future testimony demonstrates how he believed the case wasn't necessarily a 'whodunit' type of case. How could that be, I thought. Absent Lena's prearranged details, not a thread of evidence pointed to my brother as a killer.

Specifically, once Simon and his friend Ethan passed polygraphs, the information police coerced Nathan to say was no longer in line with the factual events.

Now that detectives had their backs against the wall, watching their case spiral down the drain, what do they do to find the perpetrator? Rizzuto demonstrates his efforts by forming theories and keeping with his coercive tactics regardless of the evidence in front of him.

As detectives started a third round of coercions, it was 9:00p.m. the following night. My brother was brought back to the interrogation room where he was once again cuffed to a metal ring. There was this lingering stench, a darkness, constant physical pain, lack of sleep, confusion and hunger, that hit Nathan like a sledge hammer. However, invisible to my brother was an even more detrimental threat.

"This is going to go much easier for you if you continue to cooperate," Detective Rizzuto told Nathan at the beginning of the third interrogation.

"You wanted me to say people were at my grandfather's house when I told you they weren't, and I did that. I've been doing everything you tell me to do," Nathan said with a bit of sadness in his voice.

"No you haven't!" Rizzuto said with annoyance in his voice.

Adding nothing further to the argument, Nathan's objective sense was unknowingly defeated again, without him even mentally processing the Miranda Rights he was given the day before. Nathan had bowed to Rizzuto and Summers' blatant case of police trickery. The overt measure Rizzuto engaged in to stop Nathan from intelligently invoking his rights, I later found out, was being practiced in interrogation rooms throughout our country with people Nathan's age. On the same token, I'm not so sure Nathan absolutely knew he could stop the interrogation. He may have signed a sheet of paper over twenty-four hours ago acknowledging he read his rights, but did he remember those rights? It seemed like Nathan was being pressured to continue with the interrogation which was coupled with fear, confusion, and probably just a simple willingness to do anything so he could hopefully go home. Nathan's constitutional rights were overshadowed by his circumstances in that interrogation room.

If a detective who lacks empathy can get a suspect to say one thing that wasn't true, what makes anyone believe that the same officer will go out of the way to protect a suspect's rights. The stark contrast is, a detective's job will benefit from closing a case out whether a statement is true or not. Innocent people spend an eternity fighting with the court system about the unconstitutional behavior detectives exhibited during interrogations.

By no coincidence whatsoever, detectives started out their third interrogation with my brother the same way they did during the second interview. Rizzuto mentioned that his officers had finished combing through various developments and they needed more information from Nathan. This time however, the depth of degradation Rizzuto and Summers used was meant for my brother to be continually unaware of the knowledge police actually knew was going on. Referencing the death of our grandfather to Nathan this time, the detectives left out the information about our grandfather being murdered.

When detectives asked my brother if he knew what happened, Nathan said he saw our grandfather the morning Lena came over, but he didn't see anything health wise that would suggest something was wrong. Rizzuto wasn't accepting Nathan saying this. With a face my brother characterized as someone who had a difficult time moving their bowels, Rizzuto fired-off a bunch of open-ended, vague scenarios, and innuendo surrounding the circumstances of the previous day.

Eventually, the pattern circumvented itself again and Nathan admitted to a limited role in the death of our grandfather. When he told me this, it was as if the oxygen was sucked out of the visiting room.

"The details he gave wasn't in line with the autopsy though," my mother said.

"The detectives pushed even harder," Nathan said, "for a fourth time."

They'd given Nathan another opportunity to produce a story which would be consistent with some of the evidence.

Nathan said he'd fallen victim to another bullying which again wasn't uniform with the pathologist testimony. Still, the words put into my brother's mouth, which he wrote out, wasn't to Nathan what anyone would consider murder. He was gullible and he was always being told that Lena had saw our grandfather so one can only figure that what inconsistencies there were, it all originated with her.

After three long days of trying to figure out what really happened, the detectives aimed their arrows at a target that was ignorant to his Miranda Rights. All the detectives cared about in the end were those written words they told to my brother, which was enough for them to say, "Nathan Henson, you're under arrest for murder."

8

Inspirations

After I boarded a flight and returned back home to South Carolina, I stretched out in my bed and was overcome with a bit of self-paralysis. My displeasure just kept stirring over and over and over again. My eyes stood fixed on the fan that was swishing around the tiny particles in the air, and all I could do was ponder upon what I discovered during my visit to one of Michigan's largest prisons. There was definitely a conditioned psychology behind how the lead detective had Nathan falsely confess, and it was only a matter of time until I figured out the actual methods Rizzuto employed. My brother's current position, minus evidence, was unacceptable. Why, I wondered should anyone other than those detectives have to pay the piper for the manipulation that brought about fallible information. To unveil the points I was unaware of, I needed to seek the perspective of someone at the actual trial.

Interestingly enough, my grandmother, who was still living with my sister and I, had herself been a part of the group of family and friends who went to support Nathan throughout the course of his two and a half week trial. As soon as I took note of her presence inside Judge McDonald's courtroom, I went to go see what her impression of the arguments were.

A short walk down the hallway where we had arched doorways and architectural embellishments that made graceful transitions to each room, I stepped inside my grandmother's precisely planned space. She was busy emptying a dresser drawer for a vacation to Switzerland, where she was going to visit some of our relatives. Most eager to get her conclusion about the legitimacy of the jury's decision, I asked my grandmother her opinion of Nathan's trial.

"If you do decide to pour your heart in this you should keep a journal of everything you're doing. And your position will have to be presented well so people have an emotional response," my grandmother explained.

"Can you play devil's advocate grandma? Give me reasons outside of the confession that you believe persuaded the jury?"

Her expression, to me, came off as if she was not immediately available to discuss Nathan's case. Nonetheless, she exercised a pause in putting the clothes inside her luggage, then went and sat on the cushion top resting across the ledge of her bay window. She never got tired speaking about life stories, and it was clear that my initial impression was wrong because at that moment she'd gotten comfortable to have the discussion I wanted.

"I started to notice the trial taking a turn when I looked at one of the jurors' face during that detective's talk about Nathan's second statement," she stopped her sentence to take a backwards shift in her seat. "But, there were also a few pieces of evidence I didn't really understand."

Before pulling the lid off the points of debate, my grandmother undertook the argument which serves as the basis for most prosecutions in America. What was the motive?

The theory of money being the sole foundation of the state's claim, made sense. The ingredients of the poisoned motive would be correct only if Nathan didn't know how to gain possession of Lena and our grandfather's joint money. From the time Lena had begun making herself known to everyone in our family, Nathan always visited, and spent the night on Timberline quite regularly. Ever since Simon and Nathan worked in tandem together, they'd always been aware of where our grandfather kept everything valuable. This included keys to safes around the house, jewelry, cash, checks and credit cards.

I can remember Nathan coming home after visiting our grandfather, showing our parents invoices where Lena was racking up serious debt using our grandfather's credit. Twenty to thirty thousand dollars alone was accumulated at Victoria's Secret. People talk about out of control prolific government spending, well, Lena had turned into a prolifiteer unleashing a carnivorous scheme of the same caliber. The only difference, she didn't have stake holders to worry about. The fact that the state was trying to say Nathan did this horrendous crime to our grandfather for money he knew how to access, was absurd to us. As I knew though, the fact that Nathan from his very first statement admitted to forming a plan to take from Lena what she was swindling our grandfather out of, that didn't look good.

The words of what some describe as my brother's valiant plot, allowed the state to introduce into evidence a document where Nathan was listed as the culprit of having forged a check on our grandfather and Lena's bank account months before. The amount was for a minuscule dollar sum, but under the similar allowances, the prosecution proposed to the jury that Nathan would go to great lengths to take what was not his.

"But didn't the prosecutor supposedly mention to one of Nathan's attorneys that the case was weak? So I don't understand his argument," I said to my grandmother, referring to my mother's statement back at the prison.

"That's the first I've heard of that, but there was also an issue with some items found on your brother when he was arrested."

Through police testimony, my grandmother pointed out a wish list that had Nathan's fingerprints on it. It was found in a back pack, and was also linked with the alleged motivation for murder. My brother's attorneys railed against the state's ill meaning of this list which had, 'Get another job,' listed as number one. Nonetheless, prosecutors contended my brother's wanting to get another job was nonessential when they reduced the entire list down to its common denominators. Under Nathan's desire to align his future with different employment, was him wanting to get another BMW. He also listed wanting to get another apartment. The last itemized thing on the wish list, Nathan included wanting to get his license cleared up. In company of this priority list were a few other possessions in a standard size envelope which was found in Nathan's pocket when he was arrested.

Jumbled together in the opening of the envelope, was a Marshall Fields' credit card, a gold Chrysler retirement card, an affidavit of forgery, and a newspaper article about how our grandfather received millions in his settlement. While each of those objects did belong to my grandfather, my grandmother told me it was worth pointing out how those facts gave prosecutors tremendous satisfaction. They'd believed it would show additional desperation on the part of Nathan.

While the state seemed to have created a scenario that would convince many, I'd remembered reading the truth, and it made me feel somewhat relieved. As it turned out, in

Nathan's first, second, and third statement, he told detectives Lena handed him some kind of envelope with things in it. Instead of the usual satisfied feeling prosecutors get when presenting evidence they claim to be so sure about, my grandmother said she analyzed the dynamics carefully. She couldn't say with certainty that the jury took their time to weigh all the evidence.

"I don't think your grandfather's belongings being found on Nathan was that big of a deal because they found credit cards with your brother's name on them in his own wallet."

"What could he have done with... what did you say – a Chrysler retirement card, a newspaper article and an affidavit. He couldn't do anything with any of that stuff."

"Here's one of the major problems I had with his court process," the hue of my grandmother's face seemed to change as she continued. "There should have been some attention given to the fact that one of the jurors said Nathan should have testified. Then you had the other juror...she was falling asleep most of the time."

At the peak of my grandmother's recollection, she touched base on the state witnesses. "Many of them had a particular change in their mood," she said, "It was always when Nathan's attorneys questioned their investigation."

One after another, each expert and detective, sat on the stand and perpetually espoused a hostile rebuttal to each defense question. Nathan's defense team was just simply trying to get clarification about certain facts.

"Too often," my grandmother said, "it was exasperating to see the clear divide of such truth finding."

Detective Rizzuto had a sharp tongue with his responses. The pathologist, Dr. Drags, was an expressive face man who flaunted his work of the case with a bit of an aggressive stance. The dismissive evidence technician, who said cost was one of the factors as to why the state did not test certain pieces of evidence, she showcased her allegiance to the state with a façade to say she didn't understand a lot of my brother's defense attorney's questions.

"They all put on a stage performance to say the least," my grandmother said.

While my father's mother didn't want to believe race was a contributing factor during the balancing of competing interests, she explained, "It was definitely unequaled compared to the counterparts of our class."

With a sober approach, most suspects in custody are thrown to the evil institutions where law officials perpetuate the use of rude, crude, and senseless practices protected by loopholes in the law. Perhaps, my grandmother said, if Nathan knew what was going on he wouldn't have been under the coercive pressures of Detectives Rizzuto and Summers, who kept insisting to Nathan what they wanted to hear.

The instant my grandmother finished giving me a refined disquisition, I saw to it that my devotedness leveled towards finding time to read more of Nathan's transcripts. Before then, I heeded the warning given to me. I had to take time to enrich my life with timeless truths of my own.

As I jumped into the great unknown, before school started again, I enjoyed my summer having no boundaries. I'd wake up at the crack of dawn practically every day and looked for new experiences. I aligned myself with a traveling baseball team where I played the position of an outfielder. I activated a social relationship which brought into fruition, a first love. I developed a fierce appetite for a variety of cultural exhibits, ethnic restaurants, and I partied hard at a few night clubs for teens my age. Amidst all my unlocked potential, alongside the unbreakable friendships I'd managed to develop, I made an equally important leap with sustaining a job at an Italian eatery just so I could show some independence and save up for the mission I always had my mind set on.

The main take-away of subjecting myself to a drove of opportunities, was my absence of finding transformative methods to get Nathan back to the place I knew his heart thumped strong for. While I had undeniably stepped away from the cause for way too long, I quickly got used to the hectic pace of my eleventh grade schedule, then resumed discovering the seeds of conflict my grandmother and I discussed.

When I picked my leather journal up from the warm window ledge it sat on all summer, some of the dust lifted. I wiped my hands across the football textured top then opened the recorder and read the last entry I wrote:

> **An entire army against my only brother.**
> **How noble is that when they refuse to prove**
> **he did anything. What inconsistencies can**
> **break apart the charging opposition?**

Not once did I question the premise of that inquest. I knew exactly where I had left off.

I sequestered myself in our study room and begun outlining a series of replies to the questions I felt no one played an aggressive role in finding. Each issue I ran across, where I checked its' validity, over and over throughout a four-month span, couldn't be subject to anything other than a clear interpretation. Some of the developments that were new to me, were clear in court documents. There were a few issues that stood out which I was already aware of, and I wasn't so sure the jury considered those situations.

First, I viewed the coroner's failure of not estimating a time of death to be ridiculous. Even paleontologists who discover prehistoric life can determine about when a fossil was deposited. Dr. Drag testified as to the time of death being 'unknown.' He was sure though, the date of death was December 2, 2002. The discrepancy with those so called reliable generalities is, Nathan's confession mentioned the altercation causing our grandfather's murder happened the evening before the actual date of death. Is it plausible to say Nathan purposefully changed the date of the crime? Or was Nathan simply using the date detectives were telling him the crime occurred? Either way, Nathan did not know that it was a murder.

Eight to twenty minutes. According to microscopic sections of the brain, which indicated hemorrhaging went on, that's how long the Chief Medical Examiner said my grandfather's brain was deprived of oxygen. With no reservation, I shuffled through the huge stack of papers and located something I remembered my grandmother and I talking about. In Nathan's first statement, where under the best efforts it can't be contradicted, he was clear-eyed about having seen Lena go to our grandfather's room and stay in there for twenty minutes or better, with the door shut. There was also the fact that my brother told police he didn't know why Lena was bleeding so much. Lena testified that she never went into the ensuite bathroom where her blood was allegedly found.

The chronicling of this sinister phenomenon also goes to show that some type of physical encounter in the form of a struggle happened between my grandfather and the perpetrator. What was important to note was, if the suspect got scratched, or when the killer put their arm around my grandfather's neck like the coroner suggested as one of the possible acts to have caused the murder, their skin tissues might have been deposited underneath my grandfather's fingernails... vice-versa as well.

"The first thing a person is going to do when an arm is placed around their neck is pull it off," Detective Rizzuto declared to the court.

Amongst ninety-eight percent of cases, fingernails are non-contributory, the pathologist asserted, but he submitted the clippings anyway. Was it non-contributory because detectives sought to get confessions so that the department wouldn't have to spend their budgetary funds on DNA testing?

Continuing on about the basics of collecting evidence, the pathologist discloses how fingerprints are transferred onto a deceased persons skin. While my grandfather was found in nothing but a t-shirt and boxers, there was the possibility of DNA and fingerprints being present on him. The pathologist on the other hand said the process to obtain such evidence on a body had to be done at the crime scene. That wasn't done.

However, the Michigan State Police laboratory in Northville, tested a wide range of those materials related to my grandfather's death. Including, the blood found in my grandfather's bathroom, which was determined to belong to Lena. Despite this finding, the clothing my grandfather was wearing was not preserved. Why would they throw away what he was found in? Most importantly, it was unreasonable and absurd for detectives to make the decision not to test the fingernail clippings, the comforter, or the blood on the floor that sat directly by the bed my grandfather was found hidden behind.

In the thick of the state's fight, they presented testimony from a technician who searched the Jeep Nathan went on a high speed chase in. She told the jury that my grandfather's driver's license was found in the center console. In my heart of hearts, I believe the technician stood firmly to this position because the state was arguing how Nathan needed our grandfather's identification to take his money. The reliance on those alleged facts was tampered with when Detective Rizzuto testified about the identification being found on a table in the master bedroom.

"That's how we made a positive identification of the victim." Rizzuto insisted.

Though there were no signs of my grandfather being bound and gagged as Lena had indicated in her audacious claims, two kinds of restraints were found in her Jeep, tucked in a bag belonging to my brother. Lena had ample enough time to plant those items in that bag, Nathan's attorneys argued. She could have done so when my brother stopped at a gas station and went in to pay for gas. But then there was a part of Nathan's first statement that had me re-evaluate whether the killer was someone no one thought to look at. Nathan mentioned to detectives that when Lena was at the front door, he also heard someone coming in through another exterior door on the Northeast side of the house. Was someone already there with Nathan, I wondered? Or did Lena actually bring someone with her to the house? Under either scenario, there would be the opportunity for other individual(s) to have killed my grandfather.

On my final peruse through the thick case file, there remained another mystery. The blue knit hat, with handmade eyeholes, found next to a short curly hair on the bathroom counter – it was never determined who it belonged to. I was confused to have found obvious facts prosecutors deviated from. My next move was to identify case law, and science regarding the processes correlated with young innocent lives being coerced into false narratives. These practices are never beneficial for the victims.

Due process commands that no man shall lose his liberty unless the government has borne the burden of producing convincing evidence to go before a jury. The values our forefathers built this country around seem to be difficult for too many law authorities to retain and apply even when our very own capitol hill is under siege.

In favor of not having to turn over every stone in serious cases; in favor of some officers' social, economic, gender, and racial biases; many who are appointed to enforce the law, use their training hazardously, and for what?

9

Enlightening Arguments

In the passing months, I was completely surprised when I came home and saw a sizable package sitting on my front porch. I'll never forget that day because I was extremely excited about Nathan sending me a gift without there being a momentous occasion. Inside the box was a hand carved wooden chest board, a card, and a letter. At first view, his writing appeared out of the ordinary. When I began reading the second paragraph of his written expressions, my heart sank. As I read his words he presented a clear resistance to the Michigan Court of Appeals' decision to affirm his conviction. With anticipation, the family waited for a decision to the Motion for Reconsideration. Unfortunately, it wasn't long before Nathan received yet another denial. Undoubtedly, anyone who can withstand such denials, comes out stronger on the other end.

After reading only a few paragraphs of Nathan's dramatic letter, my eyes continued gliding along the crowded words. Unexpectedly, I'd generated in my mind, these vivid images of him writing what I was reading. Nathan was sitting in his Level IV, one-man cell, guiding his pen from left to right on the lined paper. With each pause, he focused his eyes forward through the bars. Having a front row seat to the muted, back cat-walk, an officer would occasionally come by and leer closely into his cell. If it wasn't for the sparse lighting outside his front bars, he'd find himself entombed in a darkened concrete shelter, listening to a bunch of condemned inmates yelling and screaming vulgarities all day long.

I could tell by the tempo of Nathan's language that he was mentally doing all he could to triumph over the great misfortune in his life. Nathan was now faced with making the decision to further his urgent arguments to the Michigan Supreme Court and the Federal Courts. In the process of developing the framework for his supporting contentions, money for legal representation, legal copies, and just basic living essentials started to become thin.

The welcomed relief he relied on from Franck, was unexpectedly affected by Hurricane Katrina, which brought ruin to all of New Orleans. When our mother mailed Nathan a card explaining the news about his family members having had to be rescued by the Coast Guard during this storm, he immediately put in place a proactive plan to sustain his lifestyle within his confines. The first thing he was clear about doing was letting go of his defiant position about not wanting to work with convicts that he had a flawed opinion about. Regardless of Nathan not having interacted with most inmates observing these individuals on the yard, he felt was something that needed to be done to get some kind of understanding about their characters.

Even more perturbing was Nathan being required to work. The one-man director responsible for placing every inmate into a required school program or job, hired my brother as what they call in prison, a unit porter. For the very people he had such disdain for, Nathan had to clean up behind them. The place was not always riddled with filth, but the most atrocious area Nathan had to clean was a space most men went in with a keen awareness. The prison showers, as anyone can imagine, is the breeding ground for a whole host of problems.

At times, Nathan regretted accepting the porter position because of the possible problems. While working, the Department of Corrections made it mandatory that all prisoners take, and pass, a vocational trade. In the trade subject of Custodial Maintenance, Nathan learned how to properly clean up and dispose of biohazard that spilled from inmates during fights, stabbings, or any other type of scenario where bodily fluids were. Nathan was taught how to handle and apply certain chemicals to different surfaces. He'd learned how to keep a tiled or concrete floor waxed, and he built the courage to learn about other areas associated with janitorial type work.

When he found out the certificate he'd worked so hard to earn was only paying wages of $1.31 for a six to eight hour day of work, it spawned him to start disobeying his jobs' rules. While Nathan did spend more time out of his cell then many others, faces frowned. The majority though, they'd appreciated him for keeping their living quarters sanitary. Nathan's modest attempt to stay to himself didn't last long. Having decided to moonlight as a typist for those who needed letters, or maybe even legal materials typed out, made the nature of his relationship with others – tolerant.

The turbulent lessons of prison he later drew on in the letter I was reading, landed him in the emergency room. It very well tore his spirit for a while. He wrote:

> ***I think they attacked me because of a disagreement I had with a guy while working. I didn't feel them hit me with***

the lock, but when I fell out I had these memories of you, mom, dad, and Isabella. We all were walking by the ocean. You know me, I don't look to be no one's enemy, and I pray that's the last time I have to experience something like that. What do you think about me asking mom and dad for the help I for so long have refused to ask them for?

Nathan went on explaining that one of the corrective actions he was taking, came in the form of him disassociating himself with any kind of work that helps the antagonistic and dictatorial attitudes around him. It sounded more to me like Nathan had inevitably been defeated by his aggressor. He'd awakened me to the cruel realities of a place that housed killers, rapists, robbers and all other non-conforming citizens that worshipped temptation. An opposing action to a non-typical situation seems likely to be normal in prison. However, Nathan's desired reaction, which I was adamant about if the shoe was on the other foot, would probably doom him to another harsh reality. Or maybe he'd even find himself in a final dead calm. It made sense to be surrounded with the necessary armored shell to preserve his own life in an environment that was out of his realm.

Following the preliminary investigation into my brother's assault, an inspector for the Department of Corrections released Nathan from the mandatory lock-down which was put in place for his security. Hours after being removed from the isolated segregation cell, the foundation Nathan had laid within his mind while living apart from general population, had quickly come into existence hours into his work detail.

"I'm sick of dealing with this job. You can find yourself

another porter because I'm not coming out to work for you people anymore," Nathan yelled when the officer gave him a direct order to begin his work duties.

His non-compliance resulted in what the MDOC called a major misconduct. He would receive a set amount of days to be spent in his cell for refusal to follow an order by a department employee.

As Nathan's journey of serving prison time was in and of itself getting more and more arduous by each day, he had a desire to return back to God. Approaching a tipping point in his letter, Nathan recited a passage that warned against forgetting God's way. People who live only for the moment while refusing to live in God's direction, need to reassess their current life and afterlife, my brother expressed. Certainly, I understood Nathan's philosophy amongst what seemed like an incurable situation he was going through. It also reminded me of how Isabella said God was a driving force in helping free those in bondage.

Shuffling the fifth page behind the yellow sheets of paper I'd already read, Nathan began the next page with a description of how sheltered he was while hunting for constant growth. Getting an understanding of how his circumstances could be viewed as a virtuous opportunity to explore himself, was difficult for me to register. Especially since I believed his mind should be focused on legal issues a majority of the day. His brain was excited at the foggy suggestions most gave him, but then there came a time when all he wanted to do was learn things that weren't on course with what I'd wished for him to engage in.

As if it was a natural born talent, he quickly picked up on sign language. Then, he applied himself some more and completed a visual graphic arts trade, where afterwards he became a tutor. His schooling and all the reading he'd done in prison was starting to give him the discipline of reflection, ideas, and theory's.

After a certain length of time, the flatteries in my brother's purposeful letter rounded off this:

> *Me being locked up I know makes you sick. I need for you to understand that self-preservation requires a list of weapons that I know you have. I want you to satisfy yourself with an independent mind. Renounce those who look to continuously create injustice using the court system. I will stand the battle of my plight, but I'm looking for you to hold your word and help get me out of here. Look over those recent opinions I mailed you and tell me what you think.*

> *P.S. Keep defining yourself. All our great freedoms are attributed to great leaders. I have faith we both can join that mighty list.*

My brother's letter woke me up. I'd deemed it a beautiful development of substance. His self-exploration had taught him to take control of all the internal and external influences while he lived under a sentence of life without parole. Nathan stood out amongst the conventional rule of thought, and enticed me to want to read a few of the powerful books he'd developed his knowledge from. Until I could make it to a book store, I knew' it was time for me to begin searching for cases similar to my brother's. When Nathan expressed that it was of the utmost importance for me to research precedent cases dealing with what's called 'Walker Hearings,' I thought about whether I could get a hold of a database that catered towards legal research encompassing the state of Michigan's criminal laws and procedures. I could balance that obligation with my mother, I knew. Meanwhile, I took a look at the hard sale for why the Michigan Court of Appeals had a restrained posture for granting Nathan any relief.

The detailed content from the panel of judges was a few pages long and they tackled the most important argument first. Nathan asserted to the Michigan Court of Appeals that the trial court's refusal to suppress his statements was clearly erroneous, and a deprivation of his State and Federal rights against involuntary self-incrimination and due process of law. It only made sense that I understand the facts of what was in debate, so I stopped reading to go grab the briefs supporting Nathan's argument.

A waiver of the right against self-incrimination, in order to be valid, must be voluntarily made, and the product of a "free and deliberate choice, rather than (as a result of) intimidation, coercion or deception." The standard case Nathan's appeal attorney listed after that analysis was *Colorodo v Connelly*. The argument was, the state's use of Nathan's coerced confession was a violation of my brother's due process right. The most damaging, was Nathan's third statement, which was not obtained by Detective Rizzuto until more than twenty-nine hours had passed after the first statement. Nathan was not re-mirandized prior to making the third and fourth statements... which was analogous to the question first then Mirandize practice - prohibited by the United States Supreme Court. It was an end-run around my brother's constitutional protections.

Argument two suggested Nathan was denied his Sixth and Fourteenth Amendment rights to a fair trial and due process of law through misconduct of the prosecutor, which consisted of improper argument and vouching for the investigating detectives.

"If it weren't for this good police work of Detective Rizzuto and other detectives involved in this, then there would be three people on trial for murder and not just one. Because of Detective Rizzuto's insistence that they get to the truth of the matter, there is one person on trial here today," the state's prosecutor argued during closing arguments at Nathan's trial.

The prosecutor also sought to sway the jury to experience sympathy, by arguing an imagined scenario.

"....He doesn't want to die. All these things running through the defendant's mind and in the victim's mind. My grandson is killing me. Horrible enough, Mr. Harrell looks up into the face of his grandson and says to himself, I'm going to die by his hands...unspeakable, incomprehensible."

In response to the allegations in my brother's petition, the Oakland County Prosecutor's Appellate Office contended that Nathan's defense team failed to show how both un-objected to remarks in closing arguments, had seriously affected the fairness, integrity, and reputation of the judicial proceedings. While explaining their disagreeable stance about the state impermissibly seeking to win the sympathy of the jury, I picked up the appellate prosecutor's brief to see how they articulated their arguments.

The art of advocacy is the art of persuasion. In closing arguments, emotional language can be an important weapon. The prosecutor, by law, can use hard language when it is supported by evidence. However, the extraneous and inflammatory misstep of the prosecutor's personal opinion, in Nathan's appeal attorneys' view, was not supported by evidence and was simply a misbehavior that was improper. The appellate prosecutor on the other hand, felt like her blatant inferences was reasonable because she had the duty to vigorously argue the state's case.

The contentions posed in the state's answer, concerning Nathan's statement, was met with a reply. Flipping to the twenty-third page of the appellate prosecuting attorney's brief, she argued:

> *When the defendant testified that he made his statements to the police because he thought it would be in his best interest, he never specified which statements he now claims are involuntary. His statements were filled with lies and they were minimizing throughout the course of his interviews.*

Following the time when I poured over the State of Michigan's attitude about Nathan's point of assertions, I picked up the unpublished findings from the Court of Appeals again. The first three sentences were the words most inmates hurried to read. If it said affirmed at the end of the short paragraph like Nathan's opinion had, most I assumed, would drop their head with fearful uncertainty. Surely, I was convinced my brother's attitude was that of a shameful and humiliated man when he saw the outcome. I can remember in an earlier letter how Nathan told me his fate had definitely been sealed. It was all because he could not, at the time, understand the mental pressures that were being put on him.

To obtain a reversal of any conviction when dealing with the appellate courts, a majority of the time there must be a significant constitutional violation, or overwhelming evidence of actual innocence. The Appeals Court concluded that the Fifth Amendment is not concerned with "moral and psychological pressures to confess emanating from sources other than official coercion." With each judge concurring, they felt Nathan had definitely made a valid waiver of his Miranda Rights. To establish this irrefutable waiver, the court said the prosecutor at trial, and on appeal, had presented sufficient evidence. Their arguments, demonstrated how Nathan understood he did not have to speak; that he had the right to the presence of counsel; and that the state could use what he said in a later trial against him.

Review of the second claim was suggested to be barred for consideration because of a procedural default. That meant Nathan's trial attorneys never objected to the prosecutor's statements in closing arguments. An un-objected to issue at trial can be a detriment to a petitioner because the appeals courts usually forfeits any alleged errors which haven't been preserved through objections. The Federal courts considered the second issue anyhow, just to see if it affected any of his substantive rights.

Although strong language was used, the judges based their opinion on the trial court's instructions to the jury. The trial court informed the jury that they "must not let sympathy or prejudice influence their decision in any way." That guidance was ruled to be sufficient for curing any perceived prejudices.

I looked back through the three-page opinion once more. By far, it was nothing that intrigued me to read again. It was basically Nathan's word during a hearing he testified at before trial, versus a detective's word who was on the force for fifteen years then. Evidently, Detective Rizzuto knew all along the courts wouldn't disturb his methods. He'd accomplished a waiver from Nathan because there was nothing to verify my brother's allegations of coercion and police misconduct. Was that also why Detective Rizzuto didn't use either a tape recorder or video recorder? Even though the room where Nathan was being interrogated in was equipped with those mechanics, Detective Rizzuto testified at the Walker Hearing about how he believed it's a very bad idea to use recorders in a course of an interrogation. For transparency I thought, why not make use of such equipment?

After understanding the courts method for determining a valid waiver of every American's Miranda rights, I considered the entire picture. I asked myself – could I or any young person remember their rights before or during a grueling interrogation when almost a day has passed? Would I, or any person Nathan's age, be able to ignore the police pressures and invoke the Fifth Amendment if we were only somewhat aware of those privileges?

The court's superior ability in viewing this evidence only disturbs a ruling if only before making a waiver, the totality of the circumstances was so much so that the surrounding facts made a suspect vulnerable to abandoning his free will. However, what happens when an intelligent waiver does occur and a suspect takes out a claim to the court that his admissions were a product of police coercion? I went further into Nathan's brief and looked for how his attorney presented case law specific to that question. Then I saw it. It was a number of factors within a distinct test which determined whether a confession was a product of an essentially free, and unconstrained choice by a person in custody.

Even though the court made their opinion as to the issue of Nathan's Miranda Rights, the passion and zeal of the state's declaration still didn't make their ruling correct. Nevertheless, I was somewhat terrified of the possibilities related to the not so good endings of challenging the values we all as Americans should care about. Is it true that the courts in our country just want to paper over difficult questions? Perhaps so! But our values stand for nothing if we don't at least try to pursue change.

10

Tactical Disadvantage

In the succeeding weeks, fall had set upon me. I was busy, once more, reading the arguments accumulated within my brother's appellate briefs. My concentration was quickly broken when I heard rustling sounds coming from the lower part of my home. I was eager to pursue the reason for why someone was creating so much noise. I inched down the wide plank stairs, rounded the end of the curved wall, and saw several pieces of luggage sitting in front of the open door. Before I knew it, the questions that lent themselves to distortions, suddenly centered towards my mother. It was definitely a surprise because she was not expected to arrive for another few days.

Despite my parents eighteen year marriage having ended in divorce, they'd agreed to hold traditional Thanksgiving dinners with Isabella and I. My mother has always been very adept at cooking, but I'd never seen her cook an entire holiday meal by herself. We all suspended work and time with friends to help with the dinner my sister and I always looked forward to. However, Nathan's absence during the holidays added to the trifecta of issues that were affecting us personally, and it had been awhile since we sat down with each other to discuss these concerns with clarity. This particular Thanksgiving though, marked a change.

After building an adequate foundation, my mother explained her concerns aloud for us all to hear. She spoke wholeheartedly about not wanting us to continuously be embarrassed to speak to other family members about their divorce or Nathan's imprisonment. At the center island of the kitchen, my dad stood on the opposite side of my mother where he listened intently to her professed beliefs. He seemed to know when she was at the borderline of cutting off her sentence, and when she did he expressed that in life our love for family should be paramount. He'd hoped our bond to one another would stand the test of any disagreements, as well as any other obstacles we found ourselves going through.

It seemed like my dad was reading my thoughts as I listened to him speak. I'd been thinking about how our family would carry on after Nathan went to prison. For those who were outsiders, they did not understand how our unity wouldn't allow for anything or anyone to bother our aura.

After out discussion, we waited for the ovens to cook the main course. In the time between, my grandmother's age-less appeal somehow or another convinced my mother to be candid about the bitter dispute of my grandfather's estate. Willing to stand in the middle and weigh everyone's differences, a mediator helped solve only but a few disagreements between my family and Lena. The probate issues that remained were being handled by one of Nathan's trial attorneys. My mother and Nathan had known him for many years prior to his representation of my brother. In fact, Nathan's attorney at one point taught a legal class my brother attended while in high school. About a year or so after Nathan's conviction though, corporate matters took precedence over the interest of my family. Needing to resolve the estate issues quickly, my family hired another attorney who'd threatened to aggressively attack everything Lena was arguing to the court.

As the open conversation kept going, my grandmother alienated the unfavorable person they were talking about, and asked about her grandson's world in the penitentiary. Nine days prior, it marked Nathan's twenty-third birthday. It was devoted towards going back to the place that gave me goose bumps, my mother explained. She reluctantly traveled by herself. This time she didn't extend her visit past a few hours.

"At first, I couldn't recognize him," my mother said about Nathan.

Nevertheless, my brother was still every bit of five feet even, had brown eyes, high cheek bones, light brown complexion, with a perfect set of teeth thanks to braces he wore during his high school years.

"What was different about him?" I asked.

My mother said Nathan was sporting a shoe shine gloss on the bald head he now had. His skin looked clear of any blemishes. His stance was as confident as ever, and he'd recently been decreased to a lower security level unit. She spoke unguarded about the order he told her he was setting down. It wasn't for reputation, but for helping those that were being ridiculed for not understanding how to combat a distrusted prison system. I was captivated at the leadership role he was beginning to take on. His influence on others came in the form of a position where he was voted in by the majority as a Block Representative. At a monthly meeting with the presiding Warden, Nathan and other inmate Representatives were responsible for coming up with solutions to the issues that affect their housing units.

Employing his understanding of prison policies and rules, Nathan also began the task of targeting the lack of prisoner health care.

"It's extremely hard for anyone to win a state medical malpractice claim," my mother explained to us.

To win an Eighth Amendment claim against a prison doctor or nurse, Nathan went on discussing with our mother how a few prisoners he knew were trying to sue the state's health care provider for deliberate indifference. Doctors at the facility he was housed at were being accused of knowing about inmates' ailments, but disregarded treatment. At the minimum, Nathan was helping prisoners exhaust all their administrative remedies before the complaining prisoners decided to file a state or federal action about the failed prison health care.

"Should we be concerned Nathan isn't focusing on his legal things?" my grandmother asked.

I sort of frowned confusingly before my mother stepped in and answered.

"He told me work as a tutor has him busy all the time."

"That's fine, but I asked about him focusing on his court issues."

"I think he's already started putting together a petition to the Michigan Supreme Court with the help of another attorney we know," I answered.

Often, the day after Thanksgiving was held to no specific play book. However, this particular year my mother and I made arrangements to go on an investigative binge at a law library near one of my mother's associates homes. The drive from Charleston to South Carolina's capitol, took us every bit of three hours. Inside the library, my mother demonstrated how to use the computer for purposes of researching anything Nathan presented to the courts. With the use of a convenient database, we were able to view many of my brother's actual court documents. For instance, I could see excerpts of transcripts and his briefs. The dates his attorneys presented documents or sat for hearings in Nathan's case could also be seen. I could read each court order in his case, and I could easily view limitless case law and other records that were associated with subjects unrelated to criminal law.

Once I reached a comfort level with knowing how to get around some of the technical snafoos my mother pointed out, we printed copies of the case law which stood behind each of Nathan's contentions. With the papers sitting on the long table, where at least six other people were quietly occupied with their systematic studies, my mother and I looked over the documents I stopped on a few days ago.

"Read that part mom," I insisted of her while pointing to an area in the case of the *People v Cipriano.*

With her soft voice, that could only be heard between her and I, my mother was in the middle of reading an important part of the case.

"The test of voluntariness is whether considering the totality of the circumstances, the accused 'will' has been overborne and his capacity of self-determination was critically impaired."

Pulling away the stapled papers she'd recited, I stretched my hand out and replaced what she read with another case. I tapped my finger on a certain section I wanted her to look over. The case of *Colorado v Connelly,* declared that there must be coercive law enforcement activity before a confession is rendered unable to use against a defendant.

For example, there are a number of factors listed from letter A through letter L, that describe what a *Walker Hearing* is supposed to resolve in determining whether a statement was coerced or not.

Those factors are:

A.	*The age of the accused*
B.	*His lack of education or his intelligence level*
C.	*The extent of his previous experience with the police*
D.	*The repeated and prolonged nature of this questioning*
E.	*The length of the detention of the accused before he gave the statement in question*
F.	*The lack of any advice to the accused constitutional rights.*
G.	*Whether there was an unnecessary delay in bringing him before a magistrate*
H.	*Whether the accused was injured, intoxicated or drugged when he gave the statement*
I.	*Whether the accused was deprived of food, sleep, or medical attention*
J.	*Whether the accused was physically abused*
K.	*Whether the suspect was threatened with abuse*
L.	*Whether any promises were made.*

My mother had forgotten exactly how the courts made this assessment during the Pretrial Walker Hearing my brother was given. So we then printed out the trial court's findings on this issue.

Despite the court's pattern of being favorable to the statements of reason given by officers, Nathan answered questions about the detectives, for at least an hour on the stand. Once he got whiff of the tempo his defense team was going to begin their questioning of him with, they'd transported his mind back to the day he'd came into contact with Detectives

Rizzuto and Summers at the Southfield Police Department interrogation room.

In review of what was said at this Walker Hearing, better known as a suppression hearing specific for challenging statements, Nathan's testimony began with him simply describing his background. Nathan told the court that he was nineteen when he was interrogated; he had one year of college underneath his belt, and; in the past he did have contact with law officials, but Nathan admitted he was not a convicted felon. He'd never been interrogated before, and his questioning in the Southfield Police Station lasted over portions of a forty-eight hour span. Although Nathan said he'd waived his Miranda Rights at the onset of his first interrogation, he'd advised the court that those constitutional provisions were not given to him on the day of the most damaging statement. In addition, the signature on one of the question and answer response sheets, Nathan strongly admitted, "Those signatures are not mine."

As his testimony continued, he'd told the court about being transported to a hospital for back, hip, and knee pain caused by the accident he was in. His testimony also revealed that the officers knew he was injured because they'd questioned him about why he was limping into the interview room. Detectives Rizzuto and Summers insisted Nathan wait until the interrogation was over before getting checked at a hospital.

Speaking to the conditions of the cell he was being housed in, Nathan testified that he did not have a mattress to sleep on, and the cell they put him in was so cold it was just about impossible for him to sleep. At the last phase of questioning by the prosecutor, Nathan bellows to the court that Detectives Rizzuto and Summers were intimidating and pressuring him to say things that weren't true.

The use of Nathan's testimony was part and partial a comforting pillow to lay down each constitutional violation on. His appeal attorney figured he'd made the correlation between the standards of precedent case law, and Nathan's testimony. For the first time, my mother read the language of the Appeals Court opinion in Nathan's case. It said:

> *"Mr Henson was a young man who the trial court deemed to be fairly sophisticated. He was fairly educated, spoke well and seemed to have a good understanding of the English language. The defendant was taken into custody in the afternoon of December 2, 2002 and his last statement was made approximately forty eight hours from his time of initial custody. The defendant was not being held absent probable cause that he committed a felony. There was no requirement that once having waived his rights, the police must re-advice a suspect of his rights every time there is a gap in questioning. The defendant's injuries were not very severe. And there was no claim of physical abuse.*
>
> *Taking a judicial note of the fact that the lead detective testified that the jail inmates were fed three times a day, there was no indications that he was in need for food. Detectives Rizzuto testified the defendant was only handcuffed to the wall when they weren't present in the room with the defendant. During the course of the interview, the detective said they did not make any threats or promises, nor did they say they used any force or coercion. The defendant did not appear intoxicated or under the influence of*

> *any substances. He did not complain that he was*
> *tired or could not answer the detectives' questions.*
> *He 'guess' he knew he could stop the questioning,*
> *and the defendant testified he thought it would*
> *be in his best interest to cooperate."*

By the preponderance of evidence, the trial judge and the appeals court ruled in favor of the prosecution. In both courts' eyes, the state had established that Nathan's statement was not coerced. Therefore, it was constitutionally admissible for the jury to have heard the statement during the course of trial.

To me, the striking role of those legal principles didn't call attention to the main case in point. It was a point that is hard to really describe if you don't understand the mechanics behind them. Did they not understand, themselves, the psychology behind false confessions? More importantly, how exactly does a person's 'will' become so overborne in an interrogation room, that they acknowledge guilt for crime(s) they haven't committed? Should we all just become complacent with the fact that someone's confessed? If we adopt those attitudes, then our innocent family and friends will continue to spend decades in prison for crimes someone else free, has committed.

On our way back home from the library, I called Isabella and told her to print out and read whatever she could find online related to false confessions. Later that evening, without the distractions of any kind of technology, we all sat comfortably on the couch in our family room and waited on my sister to tell us what she'd learned. We were all upbeat about uncovering the science behind how false confessions are induced. Our ears perked up the moment Isabella spoke:

"Many of the studies attribute false confessions to be the leading factor amongst 63% of the 113 homicide cases in the United States... where DNA later exonerated the people."

Those individuals who pleaded guilty made the decision to plead guilty to crimes they did not commit, because they didn't want to take chances in front of twelve strangers.

"Out of the inmates who do get exonerated, they stay locked up for about fourteen years on average," Isabella said.

I was grappling with that amount of years. Our ally was hope, and I'd anticipated the scale of Nathan's challenge to be resolved before fourteen years.

"What's the ethnic makeup of all the men and women who've later been absolved?" my dad asked.

While I believe race is sometimes unfairly characterized in scenarios surrounding the criminal justice system, the reality of what my dad was asking would definitely tell a tale all on its' own.

"Using the number of about three hundred people, who were exonerated before Nathan went to trial," Isabella lingered in silence while her face said she was trying to come to grips with what she'd saw. "Two hundred and five of them were African Americans. Caucasians placed second of all the wrongfully convicted. Third came Latinos, and Asians came last."

I could feel myself getting impatient with Isabella taking so long to speak about the social science on false confessions. While she spoke slowly on how difficult it is to accurately assess what she'd studied, my ability to stay focused was becoming steadily less. The leading officers in the investigations Isabella was speaking on, were unyielding about their decisions to not record the interrogations they'd conducted. Uncovering authorities best kept secrets in interrogation rooms, I'd known, created problematic inadequacies without video feed. Psychologist on the other hand, had developed ways to discover and measure distinguishable traits that expound on why innocent people confess to crimes they haven't committed.

"In a controlled experiment with some college students, psychologist discovered how people of varying ages gave into makeshift deceptions when false evidence was introduced to them." Isabella recited.

She was explaining her analysis to us like a literary professor. When she'd explain how some individuals rely on the mere belief that their innocence can be proven even if they do confess, I remember my brother voicing the same belief.

Nathan had mentioned how he had faith there would be a thorough investigation in spite of what Detectives Rizzuto and Summers were coercing him to say.

The more Isabella continued to explain the number one example for why innocent detainees implicate themselves. I was beginning to slightly understand why people would threaten their own freedom. In other words, there's a general consensus that the police will sift through all the evidence in a case, and prove a person did not commit the crime regardless of the confession.

People also become forthcoming of false evidence given to them when an interrogator reduces the significance of a detainees' culpability. A combination of these tactics are intended to embarrass and frustrate the detainee. For instance, over long periods in an interrogation room, a detainee may be presented with:

- ➢ Vague and or false information
- ➢ Constant internalization of detectives telling them they committed a crime.
- ➢ Intimidating language & body posture.

The functions of fright, deception, and show of strength wears down the will of detainee's in coercive atmospheres. Consequently, the accusatory inquisitions are compliantly answered falsely, and to the tailoring of the investigators liking.

"So...the first example you gave - It's kind of like when a detective tells you that your DNA was found in a place you know you've never been. You might keep saying you weren't there over and over again. But after a while you get so drained from their questioning that you conform to what they want to hear," I said.

"That's right!" Isabella shot back before continuing. "But what if technology wasn't available? What if there was no means of proof that could attest to the fact the DNA wasn't yours?"

At that moment, I didn't have a smoking gun answer to her question. Simply put, I surmise I would be trooped off to jail like in the old westerns. Then, I thought about her question in a reverse scenario. What if there were mechanics in place for whatever kind of proofs, but that equipment wasn't working or being used in an interrogation where police told a detainee they were? I believe that kind of deception could also bring forth a false confession. Among those dispositional influences that detainees weigh, Isabella charged us with the reality that sometimes people utter untruths for reputation.

"I assume those kinds of people want the media spotlight on them," Isabella said.

"Or maybe they just think it'll make them look cool in front of the people they hang around with," I said.

Other detainees create and or repeat lies as a need for some kind of punishment.

"Punishment for what?" my mother asked with an excited curiosity.

"It could stem from an incident that occurred prior to the time they were being interrogated." Isabella said.

The number one belief I had for why someone would falsely confess was because of mental impairment. I'd even thought of the idea of someone covering up for another person. What's also invisible to those being interrogated are short term benefits. These influences cause a person in custody to say to themselves, "Hey, I'm tired of all this confusion. I don't have any other choice but to say whatever these detectives want me to say so I can go home."

The errors that are made by police interrogators which lead to false detailed confessions, reminds me how no one really wanted to pay attention to climate change. The same, I felt, was for how the courts abandon the challenge of looking into the psychological aspects of police errors during questioning in police departments across America.

The police's reprehensible wedges break down innocent suspects' resistances. Investigators a lot of times convey or elude to the fact that a suspect can receive higher charges if they don't confess. If suspects do tell detectives what they want to hear, then by the officer's deceptive wording, they'll be rewarded with lower charges. Authorities do all of this only to obtain responses favorable to the police. The investigator may also have a suspect exercise creative control when it comes to the words they write on paper. But there's a grim face accompanied with the loud and frightening tone that's relentlessly driving descriptive theories into detainees' minds. A detainees' history of physical abuse can also be a contributing factor for why police narratives spill out from suspects' mouths.

With every denial during the accusatory and confrontational process that goes on in a small, isolated, windowless, soundproof room, interrogators overwhelm detainees' objections by literally getting in suspects' faces. As part of all their weaponry, a suspect is overtly lied to in order to force a detainee into a state of despair and confusion. This makes a person feel as if they have to cooperate so they can leave the police station like the detectives tell them they'll be able to do.

Another set of tactics that is instituted is where a detective shows sympathy and understanding. To generate a level of empathy, detectives may sometimes falsely appeal to a detainee's religion. They may even go as far as to give a compliment to a vulnerable suspects character. "We know you didn't mean to do this. God is going to get you out of this. Just tell us it was self-defense and everything will be okay."

In response to Nathan's initial appeals petition, the state's attorney wrote in his brief that my brother had the wherewithal to lie and minimize throughout the course of his interviews. If that's not a clear indication that the police were perpetuating the cycle of deceptive tactics toward my brother, then all the psychologists who've studied false confessions must be disillusioned. Apart from the cumulatively coercive methods mentioned in the Connelly and Cipriano cases, there are so many other cognitive errors that led investigators to put a bullseye on an innocent man. Simply put, the most prominent reason for this topic of discussion is because of the police's poor and erroneous interrogation training.

My family and I learned too many investigators have this opinion about how they can recognize lies and made-up stories. To ignore a claim of innocence by starting off an interrogation with the whole 'good cop, bad cop' type attitude, this can be done in error by any officer at the start of any investigation. Before I even came to understand all of what I had just excepted, it seemed implausible that coercive behavioral antics went on in the secrecy of a room where police were in charge of getting to the truth. It took the research into the definition of science, for my family and I to understand the perplexing issues which I'm sure is far greater for a lone juror to comprehend.

Miranda Rights are supposed to protect one from these persuasion techniques. But what happens if these coercive techniques are used before an officer advises one of their rights? And why not make it law to give a suspect these rights every time they're brought from a cell for questioning. What young kid or adult, who's undergoing pressures from the police, will even be considering their right to remain silent, a right to an attorney, or the right to end the interrogation?

Those fundamental rights are whisked away once the compelling influences begin. Possibly though, if a detainee saw or heard these rights at the beginning of each interrogation, that could possibly lower the rate of false confessions as well. It reminds a detainee that they have those options once more. I put emphasis on the word "reminder" because a lot of people have a difficult time remembering what someone told them an hour ago. Then again, officers down play the significance of Miranda Rights and they sometimes go further as to continue questioning even when a person has invoked their right not to speak with the police.

In Israel's legal system, the confession of an accused person isn't perceived as something significant. In fact, it's looked at as an irrational act when strong evidence of an accused person's guilt isn't present. With this phenomenon, I ask whether judges in our country will ever understand this topic.

As of 2021, Ohio and Washington have joined many other states in passing laws mandating departments and law enforcement to use recording devices for interrogations of serious offenses. In the same year, Oregon and Illinois banned police deception of young people during interrogations. This will also give an opportunity to shed light on whether a statement was actually a product of the police or the confessor. These laws are excellent improvements, and with it I still believe there will be instances where a person's decision making abilities will be compromised because of authorities' deceptive methods.

In 2012, Michigan adopted a similar law requiring audio visual recording of interrogations of all major felonies. However, failure to record or preserve a recorded statement does not stop an officer from testifying as to the circumstances and material contained inside the statement given. What's more concerning is that the requirement is considered a directive for law enforcement and its' officers, and not a right conferred on the individual being questioned for the major felony.

While our courts seem to turn their backs on experts testifying about false statements, because some may think its junk science, judges should be more open to allowing this kind of testimony. Plain and simple...judges and prosecutors can't make an accurate judgement if they don't see the interrogation. Hearing from a professional about the strategies employed during a recorded interrogation can help preserve the issue of 'he said she said.'

From the moment Nathan was arrested Detective Rizzuto saw a guilty man. He said it, "It wasn't a who-done-it type case." Those were his words. One can't argue that the objective of interrogations is to secure confessions from individuals who are guilty. So why do we constantly hear about police getting these detailed confessions from people who are later vindicated. The same mental chess game used to get actual perpetrators to admit guilt, can also cause innocent detainees to say things that aren't true.

Accusations were presented to Nathan, which later turned out to be deceptive information from an eyewitness detectives originally relied upon. I feel like this created confusion which ultimately wreaked havoc on my brother's decision making.

I believe Nathan had this naïve belief that if he admittedly minimized his culpability, like Rizzuto was blindly coercing him to do, then his actual innocence could be proven through the biological evidence the detectives spoke of. Or maybe even by the person Nathan heard coming in through the Northwest side of the house.

Clearly, testimony proves Nathan kept telling officials Simon and Ethan weren't at our grandfather's home. His compliance in implicating them undoubtedly stemmed from external influences which I strongly believe detectives covered up. Detective Rizzuto added in is testimony that there was talk of other charges. Exactly what the nature of that conversation was, no one knows, but Nathan and Rizzuto. So again, why did Rizzuto not video-record my brother's questioning when the equipment was in the room for him to use?

In short, the louder a detainee protests his or her innocence, the heavier psychological pressures are put on a person of interest. When under these stresses, all a detainee can recognize is the short-term situation they want to unglue their feet from. Thus, their decisions are not driven by ideal long-term interests. False confessions and true confessions both look alike. Particularly when there is no video of the interrogation itself. Yet, we persist in our belief that we, people who don't understand the science of psychology, can identify deception better than the next person.

If you really pay attention, it's the police who are designed to produce confessions by way of trickery, deceit, and manipulation. The law lets them do it and the law seems to care less about any type of scientific reasoning for why someone has confessed. When the police are asked to sit in front of the tribunal they hold loyalty to, to give their account of an interrogation they oversaw, what makes anyone believe authorities won't employ the same deceptive methods to the court as they use in the interrogation room. Surely the leading investigators don't want their suspect to go free. Does that answer the question of whether a member of the police department would risk their position and reputation to tell the court about their psychological coercion when a detainee can't prove such? Or are the men in blue so blind, or maybe even so misguided to believe their tactics aren't ever coercive.

In truth, evidence collected from a crime scene is what I've always thought has the best proofs. One thing I'm sure of is, Nathan and a lot of other people would not have found themselves in prison if they did not steer away from an important protection...their Miranda Rights.

11

Transparency

History seems to be replete with law enforcement strutting to the witness stands in our court rooms and proudly flexing their modes of investigation. In the instances where these overly broad sales presentations are conflicted by other reliable proofs, disgruntled citizens unify and start movements for change. Many recognize this as an assemblage of protest. In these organized demonstrations, Americans try to strip away law enforcements' immunity. We look for why some police departments use evil, coercive demagoguery to send faultless men, women, teenagers, and young adults to prison for crimes they're not guilty of. We look for the reasons why officers' actions are always justified when society sees those behaviors as crimes.

The Department of Justice I'm sure of is always inundated with these immeasurable problems. However, when it comes to the science of crimes involving false confessions, those conclusions are largely disregarded in lieu of promoting the long held belief of a party, leadership, or personal morality. Regardless of how I view the people in power, I evolved into providing a strong alliance to my brother's cause. I'd figured first it would be best to have a heart to heart discussion with a professional who had done many experiments associated with police interrogations. I estimated, whatever psychologist was willing, they would be inclined to adopt Nathan's case and use his situation as another example to showcase the validity of their science.

Nathan wanted my family and I to wait until he exhausted his appeals before we devoted time to find a psychologist who would take apart and decipher each of his interrogations.

It was senior year of high school at this juncture, and I was able to articulate with a comfortable style, anything surrounding the issues that packed over a thousand pounds on my brother's back. I wondered could Nathan argue the language in Michigan's recording laws, should be applied to him? When Michigan did adopt the like-minded initiative, would it even make sense for those provisions to be a part of the letter of the law right now, but not applicable for argument concerning cases prior to such enactment?

On a positive note, the changes send a message about how the status quo of not recording interrogations in the past, was decidedly wrong.

12

A Brazen Commitment

At every click that came after the door locked in Nathan's cell, legal work was the dominate thing he focused on in the small enclosure. With an array of constitutional arguments to choose from for his appeal, Nathan and I knew the outcome was uncertain. Having only 56 more days to submit arguments to the Michigan Supreme Court, Nathan took all of 45 days to complete his constitutional claims. The reflection of time in between was stressful. We knew there was only one go-round with the federal court. Desiring a specific outcome didn't necessarily put us in a position to receive it.

It was an early January morning and the lone letter my grandmother sat on my night stand the evening before hadn't been read. I lazily opened my eyes, then extended them wider so I could clearly read my brother's correspondence. To be modest, after taking note of Nathan's words, it seemed like he couldn't win on fair terms.

"If you want something to cry about you need to drive down to a cemetery and have a look inside," Nathan wrote aggressively.

That's a strong vision I thought. Nevertheless, there were alternate solutions. The one Nathan was going after would take a year to perfect. Forthrightly, I believe judges should not fear to change their minds after making a ruling. Some courts today though, seem to be so out of touch with the lives of the very people it's designed to protect.

Many courts don't hold much value towards those who are under guard of the state. For instance, the courts imply that ignorance of the law is no excuse for an individual whether they can or cannot afford counsel. For these prisoners who've never argued a legal position in life, suddenly they're being held to a standard where they have to understand and prepare arguments specific to the constitutional issues they face. I'm curious to know though, when two separate courts bicker over rulings and interpretations of uniformity, how does a prisoner prevail.

All throughout Nathan's appeals process, I was amazed at how he had grown to be so undeterred by all the developments which was not encouraging at all. For better or worse, my brother was wedded to another motion for relief from judgment. This time, it was to the agency that allowed snippets of the Patriot Act to be used in domestic situations just so they can tap citizens' phones without them knowing it.

A great number of Americans have good reason to believe the system by which most politicians and judges operate by, are strict constitutionalists. My brother on the other hand, stressed that I needed to be patient and not be so skeptical of the court's intentions. Of course, roles had reversed and my brother's description of the glaring prejudices wasn't as vivid as mine anymore. Nathan always used to tell me, "You can't be brave without much fear." He said it so much that I didn't understand why at times, he gave the impression of not being troubled with the courts not understanding his arguments.

By the time Nathan's Habeas Corpus petition was complete and submitted to the Federal District Court, I was graduating high school and soon to be headed off to East Carolina University. The time projected for the federal court to give a response was anywhere up to about forty-eight months, if not longer. Meanwhile, life for me changed dramatically.

First year of college was intriguing. The culture shock, the level of collegiate studies, my relentless baseball practices, and not to forget – all the fraternity parties, kept me at a hectic pace. On special occasions throughout that year, primarily holidays, I always went back to visit my brother at whatever prison the state had him at. Each time we came into contact, he still hadn't received a response. Isabella took the time out to accompany me a few times too, but she was mostly occupied with her continued schooling, as with her temporary job as a medical assistant.

Summertime the following year, still no answer from the courts. The anticipation admittedly prepared me for the beginning of each day. I relied on a few friendships to guide me towards teaching. I wanted to imprint all of what I was learning onto the youth. I didn't get to formally teach out of a classroom, but I was able to pass on my fitness skills and life skills as a gym assistant under the supervision of one of my old high school gym instructors. Then, around the time when the trees outside started to turn colors, I received the call I'd been waiting for.

"I haven't looked at it yet because I wanted you to be on the phone when I read it," Nathan said, while pulling the court opinion out of an envelope.

My heart pounded as fast as a set of pistons in an engine. I couldn't wait anymore, "what does it say?" I asked anxiously.

Seconds later, he spoke something so low I couldn't decipher what it was.

"What was that?" I asked concerned.

"Hold on Axel," Nathan roared out with frustration.

The opinion was quite descriptive, I figured. I had already sat in silence for over a few minutes. A short time after, I looked at my wrist then Nathan suddenly hit me with the news.

"I don't know what happened but...."

"What?" I asked excited but careful.

There was a lapse of about thirty more seconds of additional silence. Afterwards, I heard a crumbling sound coming from the other end of the line.

"Well, I guess I can try my claims with the circuit court and the appeals courts one more time."

"Wait a sec," I said with a tone of confusion. "Why did they deny you this time?"

Repealing Nathan's trial judge's decision at the Walker hearing, repealing his jury verdict, repealing the state's appeal court opinion and the Michigan Supreme Court ruling, was an act federal judges rarely did absent of what they construe as a 'clear constitutional violation.' Therefore, the federal court recognized no legal justification for deviating from the opinions of the courts below them.

"It just occurred to me," Nathan said, then paused. "Before I tackle another round of new arguments, I can probably look into asking the Innocence Project to review my case."

"I imagine you could probably get those fingernails and other materials tested for DNA," I said.

"Let's figure out which law schools offer programs geared towards the wrongly convicted."

"Tell you what! I'll go online and mail you a list of options tomorrow."

No sooner than the line clicked off, I did exactly what I told him I would do. Given the multitude of schools who catered to reviewing inmates' cases for evidence of innocence, I chose to give Nathan the addresses of a few popular institutions that Michigan courts were accustomed to dealing with. By the time Nathan received my letter, he'd already typed out a formal notification detailing the facts of his case. Almost two weeks later, Thomas M. Cooley Law School wrote Nathan a reply and enclosed a questionnaire attached with an authorization for release form. Less than a month following Nathan's submitting his questionnaire, a staff attorney from the Innocence Project requested copies of Nathan's trial transcripts, Police Reports, and other miscellaneous documents.

They're wanting to give attention to an inmates' case is a hurdle itself to overcome. Nathan must've elaborated with great detail in response to the questionnaire. Our family looked at this news to be a positive sign. I envisioned a fight where all hands were eventually going to make some type of personal sacrifice to see my brother free. His new found allies would inventory all the documents, then start to spread pieces of his case file all over a long stretch of chalk board. With all of Cooley Law School's student prowess, I saw the big group of young attitudes disassemble my brother's case by bolstering the use of factual findings contrary to Nathan's coerced statement. It was a picture I had in my mind every day.

Though the responsibility of each investigating student changed at a moment's notice, what was key to most was, did DNA rest underneath my grandfather's fingernails? Whose DNA was on the comforter and bedroom floor where my grandfather was found? And whose blood was in one of the hallways by a phone? These were the questions I envisioned law students asking. They had to see the blatant coercion. My concern was with how they would go back into the court and show what the jury based their conviction on, was actually a demonstration of manipulation. Had Nathan said anything in any statement that only the prosecutor would know? The answer to that, was no.

Maybe the courts would give Nathan the opportunity that Simon and Ethan had. Then again, the statute of limitations for Nathan to take a polygraph had long expired. Even though I've never heard of a polygraph test being administered for appeals purposes, I assumed maybe precedent could be made if Nathan challenged the factual basis of his constitutional issues by taking such examination. Besides, agencies of the law use them all the time when trying to decipher the truth of a matter, so why do the courts place a statutory time limit on when someone can prove their guilt or innocence.

Surely Nathan always wanted to prove to the courts that their rulings were improper. He wanted to prove that Detective Rizzuto gave testimony that wasn't in line with what happened in that interrogation room. Nathan needed to go further in his testimony about whether he could remember his Miranda Rights in the heat of being grilled by detectives. Most importantly, Nathan needed to prove to his family that he didn't do what he said he did.

Three years later, those visionary schemes of what I fancied as Nathan's utopia, was finally met with a letter by the Co-Director of Cooley Law School Innocence Project.

Dear Mr. Henson:

We have finished our evaluation of your case. After a thorough review, we have concluded that there was no biological evidence collected during the investigation of your case that would produce DNA results. While there was some biological evidence collected during the

investigation, none of it is able to be used to
indicate the identity of the perpetrator.

When Nathan finished reading the letter over the phone, he gave a forced laughter. His attempt to mask the disappointment after all those years of being upbeat, made me feel heavy hearted. Had the police thrown away my grandfather's fingernails, I kept asking myself.

In 2017, Nathan filed with the Circuit Court, a motion for DNA testing. He petitioned to have the court order testing on all the items that had blood on them which weren't tested, including our grandfather's fingernails. The trial court gave a seven page opinion, ultimately denying his motion. The court said Nathan didn't meet the threshold requirement set in the statute. That threshold being the date in which the case arose. Because Nathan's case occurred after a particular date, that was a factor he couldn't meet. In reinforcing this opinion, the court explained how there was an absence of any evidence that would suggest the untested items would reveal a DNA profile matching anyone other than Lena. My thought to that was, what if Lena's DNA was found to be under my grandfather's fingernails? Would the court still give the same opinion?

A few days after I learned of that news, I ended my work week with an attitude of a crazed author. To free my emotions, I needed to go on a full force writing spree. So here we are with "The Carnage Miranda Leaves." Leaving Miranda's protection brought carnage that can't be repaired until the courts and legislatures seriously consider the science of confessions.

In all fairness, I can say with indignation that I wish more can be done on this issue. I have come to understand Nathan's mind-set more. In the beginning years of his appeals process, he had me play a limited role for a specific reason. It was a reason I came to understand after the trial court gave its' opinion in 2017. Simply put, I was too young to step my feet into a ring of powerful men who knew how to expose my vulnerabilities. Still, Nathan was appreciative of my efforts, my loyalty, and my visions.

These life events are being shared with the purpose of orientating a massive shift in the way we think about people who confess. False narratives are disproportionally influential to jurors' verdicts. Even with that in mind, the broadly accepted police tactics frequently tend to handcuff our teenagers and young adults to the customarily obscurities of an interrogation room. Mainly, it's because the disturbing behavior inside those rooms aren't being recorded. Can you picture your child being put through exhaustive rounds of bullying, threats, promises, and false acts of leniency just so detectives can get them to admit to acts someone else committed.

If this story is not enough for a conversation to be had, then try looking at the dramatized cases of The Central Park Five, The Norfolk Four, The Birmingham Six, and the Guilford Four. If that's not enough, I suggest researching the data involving false confessions. When the data is revealed, go find out what's being done to make a change.

The core of this, once freehand text, is meant to show Americans how our chances of coercion is tremendously increased when we decide to kick Miranda to the curb. The effects of police coercion is deeply embedded in America's dark past and amongst the present. The psychological portrait of someone being interrogated, mostly depicts how authorities subvert a detainee's will power. Another culprit for which responsibility can rest on is the surge of hidden biological forces that only psychologists can offer explanations about. Without their science, the response to those who confess, whether falsely or truly, will be based on feelings. The intellect of how our brains can be high-jacked by stressful circumstances needs to take the place of what judges and prosecutors think or feel.

Once someone has repetitively tried to compel you to swallow their beliefs, an over stimulation of dopamine occurs in our brains. When this happens, we become deficient in logic. I suggest as a nation we do away with the silence and address the issue of safeguards in interrogation rooms as diligently as we do with police brutality. There's a need to review those cases where police made the decision not to record. Psychologists should also assess those interrogations using transcripts, police reports, and statements given by the detainees.

Another meaningful necessity is the duty to teach our coming generations how to mitigate the risks of police manipulations when being interviewed. In not doing so, our lenses will continue to see a court system that will rule against claims of coercion at the same rate police shootings are being justified. In the years to come, watch and see, we will see a host of other individuals being exonerated after having confessed to crimes they did not commit.

The communities of America, through today's pandemic, have begun learning how to extract treasures out of tragedy. We've started learning how to find a room to amplify our voices in. We've also learned how to stay amongst those people who our concerns resonates with. Extracting opportunities to make changes in laws that can have an effect on so many, seems to be on the rise. Yet, even those who aren't confined to a cell with detectives using manipulative strategies on them, are being coerced to do things they would rather not do.

Today, when we look at our states, our government, and the institutions associated with either, many of them give value to vaccine requirements and mask mandates for fighting Covid-19. Other issues like parents being threatened at school board meetings, critical race theory classes in schools, voter rights suppressions, and employee walk outs because of controversial opinions, all pressures people to come in compliance with a position. Another option, of course, is to complain and try to make change. In certain political areas though, voices that try making a change, they get muted. The suggestions they are giving ultimately amounts to threats. Then what happens, you either comply, or you put what's being threatened on the line.

Ultimately, we all live in a climate of fear. For many of us, we're scared and refuse to be indoctrinated into extreme ideas and circumstances that's not consistent with our own beliefs. However, that comes with a price sometimes. For those that perpetuate self-interest tactics and manipulations to advance a satisfaction of whatever kind, primarily for order I believe, then there will always be irreparable damage. The complexity of our society is unraveling so much, many can't resist the pressures of those entities they rely on for maintaining the American Dream. Others, they comply just to stay afloat.

Finally, as I round the bend towards my conclusion, I remember my pulse quickening when I would press my pen down and write on this subject. The searchlight I've shined through all the investigation I've done, has given me a vantage point to see injustice drooping ominously from the cracks of this country. Nothing matters more to me than to see Nathan and the many who are similarly situated, emerge from their situations. Equally, If you are one to believe such, the hunt for who should be in Nathan's place, I'm sure isn't all that hard to figure out.

My remembrance of the infinite sobs at my grandfather's funeral, frightens me beyond feelings. My mother's soul cringing shrieks after hearing the jury tell her son he was guilty, echo's in my mind always. On other occasions my conversation in those prisons, and during each fifteen-minute call my brother makes to me, turns out to be extremely painful.

What I believe to be the court's miscarriage of justice, has infringed so much on my brother's freedom that they literally have stake on him until death takes over his body. Even then, they will handcuff his lifeless body to a stretcher and transport him to the nearest morgue. No one in their right mind can tell me that's not a repressible image. So I've took this exploration into both our young lives, then, so I can place his broken liberties into the spotlight. From this moment forward, my family and I are curious to see how the people of this nation will respond to a tale that must be continued on.

Moving forward I'll explore how judicial interpretations are geared towards making people believe protections are for suspects and defendants. When in reality, those protections and so many more are purpose driven for permitting the "state" to: obtain and use false confessions; refuse to test DNA when identity is at issue; and refusing to permit polygraph examinations. If you look at *Miranda V. Arizona,* which was decided in 1966, it has not been revisited in the last six decades. Instead, the only developments have been to allow the "state" more opportunities to subvert *Miranda's* original intentions. Cut outs have been created that gives law enforcement the discretion whether or not to record an interrogation. If that's not a Fox being in charge of a Hen house, then I don't know what is.

To Nathan – this my brother is just a small step towards the mission our family will never give up on. There's still so much left to be done.